PATHWAYS TO HOLINESS

Louis of Granada

━━━━━ ◆ ━━━━━

PATHWAYS TO HOLINESS

Translated and adapted by
Jordan Aumann, OP

ALBA·HOUSE   NEW·YORK

SOCIETY OF ST. PAUL, 2187 VICTORY BLVD., STATEN ISLAND, NEW YORK 10314

ST PAULS

This book contains selections from Volume 2 of *Summa of the Christian Life*, translated from the Spanish by Jordan Aumann, OP, and published by TAN Books, P.O. Box 424, Rockford, Illinois 61105.

Library of Congress Cataloging-in-Publication Data

Luis, de Granada, 1504-1588.
   [Obra selecta. Volume 2. English. Selections]
   Pathways to holiness / Louis of Granada; translated and
adapted by Jordan Aumann.
     p.   cm.
   Contains selections from Obra selecta: una suma de la vida
cristiana, v. 2, translated by Jordan Aumann.
   ISBN 0-8189-0805-X
   1. Christian life — Catholic authors — Early works to 1800.
2. Catholic Church — Doctrines — Early works to 1800.   I. Aumann,
Jordan. II. Title.
   BX2349.L843   1998
   248.4'82—dc21   97-36682
                                        CIP

Produced and designed in the United States of America by the
Fathers and Brothers of the Society of St. Paul,
2187 Victory Boulevard, Staten Island, New York 10314,
as part of their communications apostolate.

ISBN: 0-8189-0805-X

Printing Information:

Current Printing - first digit   1 2 3 4 5 6 7 8 9 10

Year of Current Printing - first year shown

1998   1999   2000   2001   2002   2003   2004   2005

Contents

v

Biblical Abbreviations

OLD TESTAMENT

Genesis	Gn	Nehemiah	Ne	Baruch	Ba
Exodus	Ex	Tobit	Tb	Ezekiel	Ezk
Leviticus	Lv	Judith	Jdt	Daniel	Dn
Numbers	Nb	Esther	Est	Hosea	Ho
Deuteronomy	Dt	1 Maccabees	1 M	Joel	Jl
Joshua	Jos	2 Maccabees	2 M	Amos	Am
Judges	Jg	Job	Jb	Obadiah	Ob
Ruth	Rt	Psalms	Ps	Jonah	Jon
1 Samuel	1 S	Proverbs	Pr	Micah	Mi
2 Samuel	2 S	Ecclesiastes	Ec	Nahum	Na
1 Kings	1 K	Song of Songs	Sg	Habakkuk	Hab
2 Kings	2 K	Wisdom	Ws	Zephaniah	Zp
1 Chronicles	1 Ch	Sirach	Si	Haggai	Hg
2 Chronicles	2 Ch	Isaiah	Is	Malachi	Ml
Ezra	Ezr	Jeremiah	Jr	Zechariah	Zc
		Lamentations	Lm		

NEW TESTAMENT

Matthew	Mt	Ephesians	Eph	Hebrews	Heb
Mark	Mk	Philippians	Ph	James	Jm
Luke	Lk	Colossians	Col	1 Peter	1 P
John	Jn	1 Thessalonians	1 Th	2 Peter	2 P
Acts	Ac	2 Thessalonians	2 Th	1 John	1 Jn
Romans	Rm	1 Timothy	1 Tm	2 John	2 Jn
1 Corinthians	1 Cor	2 Timothy	2 Tm	3 John	3 Jn
2 Corinthians	2 Cor	Titus	Tt	Jude	Jude
Galatians	Gal	Philemon	Phm	Revelation	Rv

Translator's Preface

THE THREE VOLUMES of *Summa of the Christian Life* were originally compiled by Father Antonio Trancho, O.P., of Almagro, Spain, and published in 1947 under the auspices of Bishop Francisco Barbado, O.P., of Salamanca, Spain. Unfortunately, Father Trancho did not live to see the publication of his work, because together with twenty-six fellow Dominican priests and seminarians, he gave his life for God and for Spain when the entire Dominican community was murdered by Spanish Communists during the Spanish Civil War.

This new edition of selected passages from the *Summa of the Christian Life* is made possible through the gracious permission of Mr. Thomas A. Nelson of TAN Books and Publishers, P.O. Box 424, Rockford, Illinois 61105. However, the selections in this present volume are not a literal repetition of what previously appeared in *Summa of the Christian Life*. The text has been adapted and re-arranged, and new material has been inserted whenever a more detailed explanation or an updating was considered necessary. The three-volume set of the original English version is still available from TAN Books. The contents of this present volume are drawn from the following treatises composed by the Venerable Louis of Granada: *Introducción al símbolo de la fe; Compendio de la doctrina cristiana; Guía de pecadores; Libro de la oración y meditación.*

Louis of Granada stands without a peer among Dominican ascetical writers and his works are known and loved throughout the Christian world. He was a contemporary of St. Teresa of Jesus, St. John of the Cross, St. Peter Alcántara, St. Francis Borgia and St. John of Avila, all of whom lived in the Golden Age of Spanish spiritual literature.

The spiritual teaching of Louis of Granada received official approbation from the Council of Trent and Pope Paul IV. Later, as he was approaching the end of his life, he received a personal letter of commendation from Pope Gregory XIII, who praised "the sublime doctrine and practical piety" in the sermons and writings of the humble Dominican friar.

Together with St. Francis de Sales (1567-1622), Louis of Granada is aptly described as a theologian for the laity, although during his lifetime he was disdainfully dismissed by some of the elite intellectuals as an author who "writes for the wives of carpenters." Bishop Barbado of Salamanca has stated that those critics seem to forget that "the wife of [Joseph] the Carpenter was full of grace and blessed among women."

When the Second Vatican Council reminded the Christian faithful — laity as well as religious and clergy — that they have an obligation to strive for the perfection of charity (*Lumen Gentium*, 40-42), it was simply repeating the teaching of Louis of Granada, St. Francis de Sales, and Christ himself. The spiritual doctrine in this book is the traditional Catholic teaching expressed by St. Paul: "For this is the will of God, your sanctification" (1 Th 4:3).

Jordan Aumann, O.P.

Biographical Note

On January 2, 1492, Spain was liberated from the rule of the Moors and united as a single nation under the Catholic rulers, Ferdinand and Isabella. Spain had been under foreign domination for eight centuries (711-1492) but had kept the faith throughout the long period of subjection to the Muslim rule emanating from the Alhambra in Granada.

In October of that same year, thanks to the support of Ferdinand and Isabella, Christopher Columbus set foot on the shores of the New World, thus opening the door to the golden age of Spain. Twelve years later, Louis of Granada was born in dire poverty to a young couple who had only recently migrated to Granada from Galicia in northwestern Spain.

A few years before his death, Louis stated in a letter to his good friend Charles Borromeo: "I was the son of a woman who was so poor that she lived on the alms that were given to her at the gate of the Dominican monastery." It was in that same monastery of the Holy Cross in Granada that Louis was clothed in the Dominican habit on June 15, 1524. The monastery had been established by Ferdinand and Isabella because of their devotion to St. Dominic, founder of the Friars Preachers, and as a gesture of gratitude for the services rendered to Catholic Spain by Fray Tomás de Torquemada, O.P.

In those days a poor boy had limited options from which to choose a career. He could enlist as a soldier in the service of the king, he could serve the Church as a religious or in the diocesan priesthood, or he could work his way across the ocean and seek his fortune in the New World. Louis chose to enter the Order of Preachers in the Dominican Province of Andalucía, with headquarters at Granada.

This Province had been established in 1515, and in the ensuing years it had sent so many friars as missionaries to the New World that at one time all the Dominican houses in Latin America were under the government of this Province. In that early period the mendicant friars — both Dominicans and Franciscans — were outstanding missionaries in South America, the Caribbean and Mexico, branching out from there to the Philippines, China, and Japan. In time the Augustinians and the Jesuits would also contribute heavily to the evangelization of the New World and Asia.

At the age of twenty-five, Louis was sent to study at the famous college of St. Gregory in Valladolid. After five years of residence in the invigorating climate of Castile, both his professors and his confreres looked upon Louis as a very promising professor of theology. Louis, however, was not interested in spending his priestly life as a teacher, and when the call went out for volunteers to establish a new Dominican Province in Mexico, Louis was among the first to step forward. On August 3, 1534, he was in Seville with twenty Dominican companions to inscribe their names on the passenger list, but when the ship actually sailed, Louis remained on shore and another friar took his place.

What had happened? Previously, under Pope Adrian VI, any religious in Spain was free to volunteer for the missions in the New World, and the religious superiors were forbidden, under pain of excommunication, to prevent it. But by the time of Pope Clement VII there were so many scandals and abuses of the privilege that the pope revoked it. Consequently, the Dominican Provincial, unwilling to lose such a talented friar, sent another in his place and then assigned Fray

Louis to restore the abandoned Dominican priory at Escalaceli, near Córdoba. But Louis never lost his longing for the missions and at an advanced age he composed a catechism for the use of missionaries in the New World. Fray Louis succeeded so well in the restoration of the priory at Escalaceli that it soon became a focal point for retreats and religious pilgrimages. It was there, in fact, that Blessed Alvaro, O.P., had constructed the first outdoor Stations of the Cross in all of Europe. In time Louis' charism as a preacher and his talent for administration became evident to all, and in 1544 the Dominican Order bestowed on him the coveted title of Preacher General. Six years later, in 1551, the Archbishop of Evora, Portugal, the son of King Manuel I, invited Fray Louis to come to Portugal and explain and defend the life and mission of the Jesuits, who had recently made a foundation in that country. So well did Louis perform this service that thereafter the Jesuits were always among his staunchest friends and supporters.

Except for occasional visits to Spain, Fray Louis spent the rest of his life in Portugal, beginning with his appointment as confessor to Queen Catherine, the sister of Charles V of Spain. He was offered the title of Archbishop of Braga and Primate of Portugal but he steadfastly refused all ecclesiastical honors. He did, however, accept the assignment as Provincial of the Dominicans in Portugal in 1556.

During this period Fray Louis found time to dedicate himself to spiritual writing. After the unexpected success of his treatise on prayer (*Libro de la oración y meditación*), published at Salamanca in 1554, his writings became exceedingly popular throughout the Iberian peninsula. For example, in the period from 1554 to 1559 Fray Louis published twelve books. But his very popularity was enough to alert the Spanish Inquisition.

During the reign of Charles V in Spain the dissemination of Lutheran doctrine increased at an alarming rate. In addition to this, there was the problem of the *Alumbrados*, charismatics who were tainted with the heresy of Quietism. Unfortunately, some of the books of Fray Louis were discovered in the hands of persons suspected of heresy, and as a result, Fray Louis was accused of heresy by his own fellow-Dominicans, the Inquisitors Valdes and Melchior Cano. The latter made a list of points of doctrine on which Louis was in error.

1. He is trying to make contemplatives and perfect Christians out of everyone. This doctrine is beneficial for only a few; but for the majority of Christians it is dangerous and misleading.
2. He is teaching a way of perfection to the laity, who are not in the state of life that calls for the evangelical counsels of poverty, chastity and obedience.
3. He is guilty of errors that are manifestly against the faith or reflect the sentiments of the *Alumbrados*.
4. His teaching on vocal and mental prayer is identical with the condemned teaching of the *Alumbrados*.

If anyone was in error, it was not Louis of Granada, but his fellow-Dominican, Melchior Cano. The Inquisitor was blinded by personal prejudice and stubbornly entrenched in an excessively narrow view of Christian holiness. One wonders how he would have reacted to the following declaration of the Second Vatican Council:

> Strengthened by so many and such great means of salvation, all the faithful, whatever their condition or state — though each in its own way — are called by the Lord to that perfection of charity by which the Father himself is perfect.... It is therefore quite clear that all Christians in any state or walk of life are called to the fullness of Christian life and to the perfection of charity (*Lumen Gentium*, 11 and 40).

Many friends came to the defense of Fray Louis, including the saintly Jesuit, Francis Borgia, but to no avail. In 1559 Valdes, the Dominican Inquisitor, signed the list of books on the Index, and among them were the works of Fray Louis of Granada. Shortly thereafter the Council of Trent declared that the writings of Louis of Granada were orthodox; his *Libro de la oración y meditación* was formally approved by Pope Paul IV; and in 1562 the Dominican Order conferred on Fray Louis its highest honor: the degree of Master of Sacred Theology. It was then that his good friend, Charles Borromeo, wanted to submit the name of Louis of Granada as a prospective cardinal, but the humble friar adamantly refused.

Fray Louis passed peacefully from this life in 1588 at the age of eighty-four. The entire city of Lisbon went into mourning at his passing. In the following year the General Chapter of the Dominican Order paid tribute to him in the following words: "A man outstanding in doctrine and holiness of life, and renowned throughout the entire world."

The truth of that statement is substantiated by the fact that the works of Fray Louis of Granada are on a par with *The Imitation of Christ* as regards universality of appeal and distribution. Within a short time his major works were translated into all the European languages, including Polish, as well as Chinese, Japanese, Persian, Syrian and Turkish. They were read and praised by numerous saints; for example, St. Charles Borromeo, St. Rose of Lima, St. Francis de Sales, St. Louise de Marillac. Truly he was, as St. Teresa of Jesus described him, "a man given to the world by God for the great and universal good of souls."

Author's Prologue

J UST AS THERE IS A DIVERSITY of tastes and opinions among authors, so also there is a variety of subjects and themes which they treat. Some are enchanted by the beauty of eloquence and, consequently, they attempt to form the perfect orator, taking their pupil from his earliest years and leading him through all the steps and phases of this art until they place him at its very summit. Others use the same method to form a perfect general, a great naval officer, a competent physician, and so forth. Thus, each writer strives to explain and illustrate the topic that he has selected.

But it is certain that of all human endeavors, there is none more lofty than the formation of a perfect Christian, who is created for a supernatural destiny and lives a life that is likewise supernatural. That is why the saints refer to such a person as a celestial being or an angel on earth. And if authors have most diligently explained whatever is required for those other vocations in life, which are so much the less lofty as their goals are less lofty, how much more necessary it is to do the same for the Christian vocation, which is much more difficult to attain. St. Paul told the Colossians that the words and deeds of Christ should be preached abundantly and that they should teach and admonish one another concerning their respective duties (Col 3:16). If there is no occupation, however lowly, that does not require rules and regulations in order to be well done, how much more is this true of the greatest of all occupations, which is to serve and please God, to extend the kingdom of heaven, and to overcome the power and deceits of the enemy.

How will the uneducated know what this occupation demands of them if they are not reminded of God's promises and warnings? How will they be able to confess correctly if they are not taught the requirements of the sacrament of reconciliation and how to perform each one of them? How can they experience sorrow for their sins and make a firm purpose of amendment if they don't know the reasons for sorrow and atonement? How can they receive the Eucharist worthily if they are not taught how to do so? How can they avoid sin and grow in virtue if they know not how to recognize temptation or the snares of the devil? How can they practice prayer if they never receive any instruction? We need an education in these matters; we don't automatically receive this instruction with the grace of baptism. For many years I have desired to see a book that would treat of the formation of the perfect Christian and would contain everything that pertains to the Christian vocation. Possessing such a compendium, those who sincerely desire to serve God can find both doctrine and light for developing their spiritual life, while preachers and confessors zealous for the sanctification of souls will have a source from which they can readily dispense to such souls whatever help they need for fulfilling the duties of their Christian calling.

I am well aware that there is no lack of books of sound Catholic teaching, but most of them deal with one or another aspect of the Christian life or some particular question. They do not usually provide a synthesis or survey of the entire scope of Catholic spirituality. Furthermore, although there are catechisms and encyclopedias that treat of the Christian life, the articles are more speculative than practical; they are meant to enlighten the understanding rather than stimulate the will to the practice of virtue. For these reasons I have decided, with the help of the Lord and the writings of the saints, to compile a book in which these matters will be discussed. My purpose, as I have said, is the formation of the perfect Christian, from the beginning of his conversion to the summit of Christian perfection.

The project that we are here attempting — the formation of the perfect Christian — is properly the work of the Holy Spirit, but just as the operation of grace does not preclude our human cooperation, neither does the interior illumination from God preclude the teaching of others. And this ministry belongs especially and primarily to the preachers, confessors and spiritual directors in the Church, to whom God commits us so that we may be taught and guided by them.

This ministry is so important that Jethro, the father-in-law of Moses, advised him to delegate temporal affairs and matters of less importance to judges and other officials, but to reserve to himself whatever pertained to religion and divine worship (Ex 18:13-27). And because certain priests later became careless in discharging these duties, God spoke to them through the prophet Hosea: "My people perish for want of knowledge! Since you have rejected knowledge, I will reject you from my priesthood!" (Ho 4:6).

It is primarily the duty of bishops and preachers to instruct the faithful, but preachers are not always available nor do they always preach the doctrine that is most needed. Many of them are unable to treat of the particulars that need to be discussed when treating of moral matters; and this is due in part to the fact that the preachers themselves have not received a thorough formation in theology. Another reason for the lack of instruction from the pulpit is that some of the preachers deliberately avoid discussing certain topics. That is why spiritual reading is so important and so beneficial. Spiritual books do not bore us because of their length because we can always put them down; and they do not leave us dissatisfied because of their brevity because we can continue reading as long as time permits.

Spiritual reading has always been necessary, but it is even

more so at the present time. In the early days of the Church bishops and priests were so fervent and conscientious in the ministry of the word that preaching alone sufficed to preserve and promote the Christian life of the faithful. Today, however, many priests think that nothing more is required of them than the administration of the sacraments and the celebration of Mass at specified times. Consequently, the greater the lack of good preaching, the more important it is to make up the deficiency by the publication of good books on the spiritual life.

The treasurer of the Queen of Ethiopia was reading the words of the prophet Isaiah as he was riding in his chariot. The Holy Spirit prompted Philip to catch up to the chariot, and when he heard what the man was reading aloud, he asked him: "Do you really grasp what you are reading?" The man replied: "How can I, unless someone explains it to me?" Philip then proceeded to explain the passage, after which the treasurer said: "Look, there is some water right there. What is to keep me from being baptized?" (Ac 8:26-39). Likewise, the conversion of St. Augustine, did it not begin with the reading of a sacred book?

So sublime are the mysteries that the Christian religion proposes and so powerful are they for moving hearts that I am not surprised at the profound change that they can cause in anyone who considers them attentively. Moreover, spiritual reading serves not only to awaken those who are spiritually asleep but to safeguard the faith of those who are already awake. For that reason the word of God in Sacred Scripture is described as bread or spiritual nourishment; it sustains and preserves souls in the spiritual life just as our daily bread sustains our bodily life.

This is not a business to be hurried, but one that requires attention and deliberation. It concerns your entire life on earth and what comes after. How insistent you are that your earthly affairs be conducted with great care. You are not content with only one opinion, but will consult numerous experts lest you make a mistake. But in the business of your Christian life, you are not dealing with the things of earth but with the things of heaven and eternal life. And these things are not purely external; they touch the very core of your being. Realize, therefore, that what we are discussing should not find you yawning or dozing, like the disciples in the Garden of Gethsemane (Mt 26:36-46), but wide awake and attentive. Therefore, do not read this book rapidly, as you would a magazine or newspaper, scanning the pages and headlines quickly, with little or no concentration. Rather, sit down as a judge in the tribunal of your heart and heed the words in silence. If up until now you have gone astray, seize this opportunity to make a fresh start. Be sensible; cut the thread of your past entanglements and begin to walk in the opposite direction.

I know that I am attempting a great deal and that no amount of writing can guarantee a successful outcome. For that reason, at the very outset I beg the Holy Spirit, eternal Wisdom and divine Love, to give life and fire to my words so they will inflame the hearts of all who read them.

The contents of this book pertain to all Christians, regardless of their state of life and whether they are beginners or advanced in the spiritual life. And if it has required some diligence and no little effort to compile this material and present it in a clear and simple style, it will all have been well worth the while if the readers will derive spiritual benefit from it. No amount of physical effort can even begin to compare with the slightest spiritual reward.

- 1 -

Law and Grace

TWO THINGS ARE NECESSARY for a good life: knowledge and power. In other words, we must first know what we ought to do in order to live a good life, and then we must have the power to put that knowledge into practice by our good actions. The first thing pertains to the divine law; the second pertains to divine grace. The law teaches us the difference between good and evil; divine grace prompts us to obey the first law of morality, namely, do good and avoid evil. The law enlightens our understanding; grace stimulates our will. The law teaches us the pathway to heaven; grace gives us the power to travel on that path. God gave us the law at the hands of Moses (Ex 20:1-17), but he gives us grace through Jesus Christ, his Son, as we read in John: "For while the law was given through Moses, this enduring love came through Jesus Christ" (Jn 1:17).

We hold it to be infallibly true, as stated in the Old Testament, that God himself is the author of the Ten Commandments: "When the Lord had finished speaking to Moses on Mount Sinai, he gave him the two tablets of the commandments, the stone tablets inscribed by God's own finger" (Ex 31:18). But if God is the author of the law, it is only fitting that we should hold it in the greatest honor and reverence.

However, we may ask: What do Christians have to do with the Ten Commandments, which were given to the Jews?

We are not Jews; we are Christians. St. Paul tells us: "You are now under grace, not under the law" (Rm 6:14).

It is true that the teaching of Christ binds all Christians, but his doctrine does not nullify the Ten Commandments. Christ himself stated as much: "Do not think that I have come to abolish the law and the prophets. I have come, not to abolish them, but to fulfill them.... That is why whoever breaks the least significant of these commands and teaches others to do so shall be called least in the kingdom of God. Whoever fulfills and teaches these commands shall be great in the kingdom of God. I tell you, unless your holiness surpasses that of the scribes and Pharisees you shall not enter the kingdom of God" (Mt 5:17-20).

The law of the Ten Commandments pertains no less to us Christians than it does to Jews, to whom it was first announced. True, we are no longer bound to the disciplinary and ceremonial laws of the Jewish religion, but the Ten Commandments have not been abolished; they are still binding on all. They are, in fact, a statement of the natural moral law which governs all our actions, both internal and external. They are a declaration of God's will for us.

It should be noted that some of these commandments are affirmative and others are negative. In other words, some of them command us to perform a specific work, such as honoring our father and mother, while others forbid certain actions, such as murder, theft or lying. Note further that negative precepts oblige always and under every circumstance; for example, one is always forbidden to steal or commit murder. Affirmative precepts, on the other hand, do allow for exceptions or situations in which the law does not bind. Thus, a person is not obliged to obey one's parents if they command something over which they have no jurisdiction.

It is also important to understand that a negative precept implicitly contains a positive command; for example, the prohibition against stealing implies the obligation to respect another person's property. Likewise, a positive precept implies a negative obligation; for example, the command to honor our parents also commands us to refrain from doing them any kind of harm.

Of the two elements necessary for a good Christian life — law and grace — the second one is much more excellent and necessary, just as the spirit is more excellent than the body and the New Testament is much more excellent than the Old Testament. The reason for this is that if a person commits sin it is not because of a lack of knowledge of good and evil, for that is known to all, at least in general, by the natural light of reason; rather, it is because of a lack of control of the emotions and desires, which frequently tend to seek what is evil and reject what is good. Thus, St. Paul confessed: "I cannot even understand my own actions. I do not do what I want to do but what I hate" (Rm 7:15).

In other words, a person delights in the attraction and sweetness of vice but is repelled by the self-denial that is required for virtue, although the latter is more salutary and beneficial. Indeed, we have much greater need of the *power to do good* than the *ability to know good.* Everybody knows to some extent what is good, but not all seek the good, because it involves difficulty and self-denial. In this respect the sinner is like a sick person whose sense of taste is so dulled that he has no appetite for the foods that are good for him. And when he is told to eat this or that because "it's good for you," he will answer: "I know it's good for me, but I don't feel like eating."

The same thing is true of the sinner. He knows very well that his salvation depends on the observance of God's commandments, but he does not feel drawn to these things. He knows, for example, that charity, humility, patience, temperance, and the other virtues are good for the health of his soul, but he is drawn instead to the pleasure and self-satisfaction that come from selfishness, vanity, gluttony, lust and other vices.

But if the virtues are so much in keeping with man's nature, why is it that we find their practice so difficult? We are rational beings and the virtues are in conformity with our rationality. Then why is it so tedious for us to live virtuously and to act in conformity with the dictates of reason? It is not tedious or difficult for the horse to trot, the bird to fly or the fish to swim; rather, all these activities are a source of delight because they are so much in conformity with the nature of these animals. So why is it so difficult for rational beings to live in accordance with their rationality and follow the dictates of their conscience?

If human nature were in the state of integrity in which it was first created, it would not be difficult, but very easy and natural to practice the virtues. But we know from Scripture that man has fallen from that happy state because of original sin. He has become sick; and it is not surprising that a sick man cannot do what a healthy man does with the greatest of ease. Yes, a person in good health can do a number of things and actually enjoy doing them. He can walk and run and do his daily tasks without any noticeable effort. But when he is sick, he can do the ordinary things only with great effort, and sometimes not at all. So it is not surprising that the habitual sinner does not find joy in the practice of virtue; rather, it is distasteful to him and will remain so as long as he is addicted to his sin.

"My inner self," says St. Paul, "agrees with the law of God, but I see in my body's members another law at war with the law of my mind; this makes me the prisoner of the law of sin in my members.... Who can free me from this body under the power of death?" He replies: "God sent his Son... so that the just demands of the law might be fulfilled in us who live, not according to the flesh, but according to the spirit" (Rm 7:22-24; 8:3-4).

That is why Jesus came into the world: to heal the fallen nature that we inherited because of the original sin of our first parents. What we have lost through the sin of the first Adam, we can regain through the grace bestowed on us by the second Adam. This grace heals and elevates our fallen nature, restores the image of God within us, makes the soul pleasing to God, and infuses in us the supernatural virtues and the gifts of the Holy Spirit. And all this comes about through the merits of Jesus Christ, our Savior and Redeemer. "All praise to God, through Jesus Christ our Lord!" (Rm 7:25).

Jesus merited for us the first grace of conversion and justification, so that we are accepted by God as his children and heirs of his kingdom. In addition to this first grace, Jesus merited for us all the other graces necessary for our salvation, and to such an extent that the Eternal Father has never given and never will give any degree of grace except through the merits of the passion and death of his only-begotten Son. Moreover, a diversity of graces is communicated through the seven sacraments of the New Law, and although they have diverse effects according to the various needs of our souls, they all concur in the one common effect of bestowing grace on the recipients who are worthily disposed.

One of the basic means for obtaining grace is to ask for it from him who alone can give it. St. Paul tells us that "God is rich in mercy; because of his great love for us he brought us to life with Christ when we were dead in sin. By this favor you were saved. Both with and in Christ Jesus he raised us up and gave us a place in the heavens, that in the ages to come he might display the great wealth of his favor, manifested by his kindness to us in Christ Jesus. I repeat, it is owing to his favor that salvation is yours through faith. This is not your own doing, it is God's gift; neither is it a reward for anything you have accomplished, so let no one pride himself on it" (Eph 2:4-9).

Therefore Jesus commands us: "Ask, and you will receive. Seek, and you will find. Knock, and it will be opened to you.... If you, with all your sins, know how to give your children what is good, how much more will your heavenly Father give good things to anyone who asks him?" (Mt 7:7-10). Who could be more liberal than God, and what greater consolation could there be for us? St. John Chrysostom has said that God will not refuse his help to those who ask him for it, because he himself inspires us to ask. And what we are asking is the gift of his grace and all the benefits that come to us through grace.

And if you ask me what is grace, I shall answer you in the language of theology and the Bible: grace is a real participation in the divine life and nature (2 P 1:4). In other words, it is a sharing in the sanctity, goodness, purity and nobility of God himself, which enables us to cast off the baseness and selfishness that we inherited from Adam and put on the new man in Christ Jesus. To explain our transformation through grace, the saints and spiritual writers are accustomed to use the example of iron cast into the furnace. Without ceasing to be iron, it comes out of the furnace possessing the brilliant light, glowing heat and other characteristics of fire. Similarly, the grace infused into the soul by God has the power to transform the recipient to such an extent that he is truly divinized. Without ceasing to be a human being, he shares, according to his capacity, in the nature and life of God. As St. Paul stated: "The life I live now is not my own, Christ is living in me. I still live my human life, but it is a life of faith in the Son of God, who loved me and gave himself for me" (Gal 2:20).

Grace is a spiritual adornment that makes the soul so pleasing and beautiful in God's sight that he accepts the soul as his own child and spouse. This is the way the prophet Isaiah describes it: "I rejoice heartily in the Lord; in my God is the joy of my soul; for he has clothed me with a robe of salvation and wrapped me in a mantle of justice, like a bridegroom adorned with a diadem, like a bride bedecked with her jewels" (Is 61:10).

Grace is a supernatural and divine power that enables us to live a life that is likewise supernatural and divine. We have here a remarkable manifestation of divine providence.

Since God has willed that we live two lives, one natural and the other supernatural, he has provided two forms or principles of life, one for the natural life and the other for the supernatural life. And just as all our natural powers and faculties are rooted in the human soul, so also sanctifying grace, which is as it were the soul of our supernatural life, is the source of the infused supernatural virtues and the gifts of the Holy Spirit. These infused supernatural powers, in turn, facilitate the performance of meritorious good works. This will be greater in some individuals than in others, depending on the degree of grace that God communicates to each soul.

So great is the strength of the just soul that St. Thomas Aquinas says that the slightest degree of grace suffices to overcome all the temptations and devils in the world. The beauty and strength of the just soul are praised in the Song of Songs: "Who is this that comes forth like the dawn, as beautiful as the moon, as resplendent as the sun, as awe-inspiring as bannered troops?" (Sg 6:10).

Grace makes the good works of the just man so pleasing to God that every voluntary work performed by him for a supernatural motive is meritorious of an increase of grace. This consoling doctrine applies to all the good works performed by a person in the state of grace, even such mundane actions as eating or drinking, when done for the glory of God. If the person who performs these actions is pleasing to God through sanctifying grace, so also are the good works performed by that person.

Moreover, sanctifying grace makes the just soul a child of God and an heir of the kingdom of heaven. It is, indeed, our passport to heaven. It places our names in the book of eternal life, where all the names of the just are written. St. Luke tells us that when the seventy-two disciples came back jubilant, saying: "Master, even the demons are subject to us in your name," Jesus replied: "Nevertheless, do not rejoice so much in the fact that the devils are subject to you as that your names are inscribed in heaven" (Lk 10:17-20).

To all these benefits we may add yet another marvelous effect of sanctifying grace: the indwelling of the Holy Trinity in the souls of the just. This was revealed by Jesus at the Last Supper: "Anyone who loves me will be true to my word, and my Father will love him; we will come to him and make our dwelling place with him" (Jn 14:23). This follows logically from the fact that sanctifying grace is a sharing in the very nature and life of God; anyone who lives in the state of grace is a dwelling place of the Holy Trinity. Thus, Pope St. Leo admonished the Christians of his day: "Be mindful of your dignity, O Christian, and do not fall back into your former sinfulness."

The holy doctors and the theologians frequently speak of the indwelling of the Holy Spirit, because they are using "appropriation," which means that they attribute the works of grace to the Holy Spirit in a special way because he is the Sanctifier. Similarly, we speak of God the Father as Creator and God the Son as Redeemer, although all three Persons of the Trinity are involved in some way in the external works and manifestations of the one God.

The Holy Spirit sanctifies the soul and adorns it with his seven gifts so that it will be a fitting abode for the Trinity. But the works of the Holy Spirit do not end here. He not only sanctifies us but he helps us walk along the pathway to holiness until he has led us, safe and secure, to the portal of salvation. For once the Holy Spirit has entered the soul through grace, he does not remain idle. In the words of St. Augustine, he gives us the grace to love him, and when we love him, he gives us the grace to love him more. For that reason, theologians tell us that there is no terminus to the soul's growth in grace and charity.

The Holy Spirit governs the soul as a loving father governs his family; he instructs the soul as a dedicated professor teaches his students; he reigns in the soul as a king in his realms; he enlightens the soul as the sun illumines the world. He is a living flame that ignites our heart; a dove that makes us simple, meek and compliant; a cloud that tempers the violence of our passions; a gentle breeze that inclines our wills to the good and away from evil. As a result of his influence, the converted sinner abhors the vices that he previously loved and begins to love the virtues that he formerly rejected.

Thus, sanctifying grace renders the Christian capable of all good, smooths the path to heaven, restores and heals his wounded nature, makes God's yoke sweet, helps the individual run along the way of the virtues, makes his burden light. In addition, it infuses in the soul the supernatural virtues that illumine the intellect, stimulate and fortify the will, temper the concupiscible appetite and rectify the irascible passions.

Note carefully what God promises to do for us if we turn to him: "The Lord, your God, will circumcise your hearts and the hearts of your descendants, that you may love the Lord, your God, with all your heart and all your soul; and so may live" (Dt 30:6). But how is it that he promises to do this for us, when at another time he commanded that we ourselves must love God with our whole heart and soul? If God will do this for us, why does he command us to do it? And if we must do it, how can he promise to do it for us?

The difficulty is resolved by St. Augustine: "Lord, give me the grace to do what you command me to do and command me to do what you will." God commands us to do what we ought to do and at the same time he gives us the grace to do it. Hence, at one and the same time there is a command and a promise. God and man perform the same action together, he as the first cause and man as a secondary cause. In this regard God is like the artist who guides the brush in the hand of a student in order to help him paint a picture. Both produce the work but each contributes to the finished product in a different way. God acts with us, always safeguarding our freedom; but after the work is finished, man has no reason to glory in himself. Rather, he should glorify God in the words of the prophet: "O Lord, you mete out peace to us, for it is you who have accomplished all we have done" (Is 26:12).

PRAYER FOR GRACE AND FORGIVENESS

Great and numerous are the divine benefits and blessings, but what shall they profit me, Lord, if they do not awaken me from my sleep and call me to repent? I have been such an unworthy vessel of the grace you bestowed on me at baptism. I have defiled the temple that you have sanctified. I have erected idols of my own sinful desires and have desecrated the temple by my sinful deeds.

There was a time when I was so blind and lost that I lived as if there were no law and, indeed, as if there were no God. I gave no thought to death, judgment and the next life. The only law that governed me was the law of my own selfish desires. As a result, I have passed many years of my life in such darkness that I can exclaim with St. Augustine: "Late have I loved you, O Beauty, so ancient and so new, late have I loved you!"

But during all the years of darkness, you patiently waited, because you did not will that death should take me unprepared. How great is your mercy, O Lord! How many others have been snatched from this life in the very midst of their sins, while I, who have also been a sinner, have been spared by your mercy. What would have become of me if you had called me to judgment when I had strayed far from you? What account could I have given while in that state of sin? I surely would have been numbered among the condemned if you had snatched me out of this world during my sinful years. Blessed be your patience and blessed be your mercy!

Not only did you wait for me while I lived in sin; but by the promptings of your grace you visited me many times to call me back to your divine friendship. Frequently you reminded me of the gravity of my sins, the brevity of this life, the eternity of the life to come and the rigor of the final judgment. Even in the midst of my sins, you would suddenly surprise me with your presence. I fled from you in all the pathways of my life, but you pursued me with an everlasting love.

Dearest Lord, in spite of what I am and have been, you have infused your sanctifying grace into my soul as a sign of my adoption and a pledge of future glory. Blessed be the day that the doors of my soul were thrown open to receive the gift of your grace and the indwelling of the Trinity. On that day I was truly born again into the community of the just, through the paschal mystery of Christ and the power of the Holy Spirit. And if, as I piously hope, I am among those who are justified, I am so deeply moved that I know not how to thank you or praise you, my God. All I can do is repeat the words of the Psalmist: "How shall I make a return to the Lord for all the good he has done for me? ... O Lord, I am your servant; I am your servant, the son of your handmaid; you have loosed my bonds. To you will I offer sacrifice of thanksgiving, and I will call upon the name of the Lord. My vows to the Lord I will pay in the presence of all his people" (Ps 116:12, 16-18).

Once again, I repeat with the Psalmist: "Give thanks to the Lord, for he is good, for his mercy endures forever.... I was hard pressed and was falling, but the Lord helped me. My strength and my courage is the Lord, and he has been my Savior" (Ps 118:1, 13-14).

- 2 -

The Necessity of Faith

FAITH SIGNIFIES A BELIEF in that which we have not seen and for which we do not know the reasons for their existence. It is impossible to live without some kind of faith. St. Augustine testifies to this in his *Confessions* when he describes the state of his soul before he received the supernatural virtue of faith:

> A person who has fallen into the hands of an unskilled physician will very likely be unwilling later to place himself in the hands of even a good physician. In like manner my soul, fearful of again falling into error, refused to be cured, even though it could not be healed except by believing.... Then I began to consider the number of things I believed but had never seen or experienced, such as the events recorded in history, the descriptions of cities and places that I have never visited, and the things told me by friends, relatives, and this or that person.... Most of all I was struck by my certainty regarding the parents who had begotten me, although I could not possibly know this except on the testimony of others.... Realizing that we are too deficient and limited to discover truth by the use of reason alone, but we need the authority and testimony of Sacred Scripture, I began to understand that you would not have given such authority to Scripture unless it was your will that men should believe in you through the revealed word.

Granting that man cannot live without some kind of faith, let us now consider Christian faith in particular. First of all, we should note that there are two kinds of faith: acquired and infused. Acquired faith is that which results from the repetition of many acts of belief in facts or truths on the authority of a credible witness. This faith is a purely natural and human faith.

Christian faith, on the other hand, is infused into the soul, together with sanctifying grace, at baptism. It is, as it were, a supernatural light which illumines the intellect of the Christian and efficaciously inclines him to believe all that God has revealed and the Church teaches. The infused virtue of faith is infallibly certain because it is founded, not on the testimony of human reason, but on the authority of God himself. It treats of mysteries that transcend the powers of human reason, such as the mystery of the Trinity, the Incarnation and the Real Presence in the Eucharist. But the merit of supernatural faith lies in the fact that it prompts human reason to accept revealed mysteries that it cannot comprehend or attain by its own efforts.

The authority of God is a sufficient basis for our faith and we need not seek elsewhere for motives of credibility. St. John reminds us: "Do we not accept human testimony? The testimony of God is much greater; it is the testimony that God has given on his own Son's behalf" (1 Jn 5:9). But we should not probe the mysteries of faith that are above our comprehension. When God speaks, we should simply humble ourselves and respond, "*Credo*" (I believe).

We should also observe that since faith is the foundation of the entire spiritual edifice and the basis of our hope, the infused virtue of faith is not lost by any mortal sin except one that is directly opposed to faith. Nevertheless, the best and surest safeguard of faith is obedience to God's law and a well-formed conscience. Such is the teaching of St. Paul: "Hold fast to faith and a good conscience. Some men, by rejecting the guidance of conscience, have made shipwreck of their faith" (1 Tm 1:19).

If you were to ask me what are the principal articles of faith that every Christian should believe, I would tell you that the Church has already answered that question. In order to prevent the possibility of each individual following his own opinion or presuming to make his own private interpretation of the teaching of Sacred Scripture and the dogmas of faith, the "Apostles' Creed" was drawn up as a brief summary which each Christian can easily memorize. It consists of twelve articles of faith drawn from Sacred Scripture. The Creed itself is divided into three parts. The first part treats of God the Father and what pertains to him; the second part refers to God the Son and whatever is proper to him; and the third part treats of God the Holy Spirit and what is attributed to him.

I believe in God, the Father almighty, Creator of heaven and earth; and in Jesus Christ, his only Son, our Lord, who was conceived by the Holy Spirit, born of the Virgin Mary, suffered under Pontius Pilate, was crucified, died, and was buried. He descended into hell; the third day he rose again from the dead. He ascended into heaven, sits at the right hand of God, the Father almighty; from thence he shall come to judge the living and the dead. I believe in the Holy Spirit, the holy Catholic Church, the communion of saints, the forgiveness of sins, the resurrection of the body, and life everlasting.

- 3 -

Christian Hope

T HE CHRISTIAN NEEDS THE VIRTUE of hope because his sins have left him poor and naked and there is no other remedy but to lift his eyes to God and hope for divine assistance in the midst of so many evils, many of which cannot be overcome except by God's grace. In this tempestuous sea of life, where new storms arise every day, hope is the anchor by which we must be safely secured. Thus we read in the Letter to the Hebrews: "Like a sure and firm anchor, that hope extends beyond the veil through which Jesus, our forerunner, has entered on our behalf, being made high priest forever according to the order of Melchizedek" (Heb 6:19). The virtue of hope is one of the greatest treasures in the Christian life because it is the common remedy for all the trials and miseries of life.

But lest we deceive ourselves, it should be noted that just as there are two kinds of faith — the living faith of the just which is vivified by charity and the dead faith of the person in mortal sin — so also there are two kinds of hope: the dead hope of the sinner, which does not strengthen the soul for good works or give it consolation in its labors, and the living hope, which animates and fortifies the souls of the just.

It is about this latter hope that David prayed: "Remember your word to your servant since you have given me hope. My comfort in my affliction is that your promise gives me life"

(Ps 119:49-50). The supernatural infused virtue of hope works marvelous effects in the soul and they are so much the greater as the soul participates more intensely in the love of God through the virtue of charity.

There are four principal matters about which the virtue of hope is concerned. The first is the promised happiness of the life to come; the second is pardon for our sins; the third is the granting of our petitions; and the fourth is the assistance of God in the midst of our trials and temptations. All these things and whatever relates to them are objects of supernatural hope, and the foundation and basis of our Christian hope is the tree of the Holy Cross. And so we pray: "We adore you, O Christ, and we bless you, because by your Holy Cross you have redeemed the world."

What we hope for above all else is the eternal happiness of the beatific vision. "Now," says St. Paul, "we see indistinctly, as in a mirror; then we shall see face to face" (1 Cor 13:12). In order to attain to the vision of the divine essence, the human intellect must be elevated and strengthened by the light of glory; and in order that the divine essence may be seen as it is in itself, it must be joined immediately to the human intellect, without any intermediary. From a human point of view, this type of union is so lofty and ineffable that it would seem to be impossible, so great is the distance between the divine essence and the human intellect. Normally we cannot understand spiritual or supernatural things except through images taken from corporeal things.

St. Thomas Aquinas teaches that although the union of the human intellect with God in the beatific vision is so incredible as to seem impossible, God has produced another union that is even more remarkable: the union of God the Son with human nature. Each time we pray the *Angelus* we proclaim: "And the Word was made flesh and dwelt among us." St. John Chrysostom said that it is a much greater miracle that God should become man than that man should become God.

Therefore, since the former union has actually taken place, there is reason to believe and hope for the latter, since it is through the Incarnation that the redeemed Christian receives sanctifying grace and ultimately the beatific vision.

Nor are the difficulties any less in regard to the virtue of hope than they are as regards the virtue of faith. Just as we must exert a kind of violence on our intellects to believe that which we cannot see, so also we must do the same to our will in order to hope for that which transcends our human powers of attainment. Like Abraham, we must hope against hope, "and this hope will not leave us disappointed, because the love of God has been poured out in our hearts through the Holy Spirit who has been given to us" (Rm 4:18; 5:5). Therefore, in whom shall we hope with greater confidence than in so good a God and so loving a Father? Jesus made this same point in his preaching: "If you, with all your sins, know how to give your children good things, how much more will the heavenly Father give the Holy Spirit to those who ask him" (Lk 11:13). Indeed, is there any good thing that we could not expect from a Father who has loved us so much that he gave his only-begotten Son for our salvation?

But if God has been so generous and merciful to us, how can we fear that he will ignore our pleas? And who will let himself become so dejected in the midst of trials and tribulations that he will not be mindful of the generous promises of God and his paternal care? If this thought does not bring comfort and encouragement to the scrupulous, depressed person, is there anything at all that can do so?

We come now to a sad consideration, namely, the perversity of the human heart which, even as it relies on this great virtue of hope, still persists in its sin. If you were to ask any of these habitual sinners how they can hope to be saved, they would say that they can be saved through faith in Jesus Christ and hope in the merits of his sacred passion and death. It is true, of course, that the passion and death of Christ is at once the greatest motive for hope and the greatest stimulus for fear of the Lord. But some stubborn sinners pervert it and use it as an excuse for continuing to sin.

This is a deception of the devil, the father of lies, who tries to use good things for an evil purpose. The devil knows that all men, however sinful they may be, desire to be saved and be happy for all eternity. So he comforts the sinner by saying that Christ has already atoned for sin; the price of redemption has been paid. It is as if one were to say that the Son of God came down to earth in human form, and suffered and died so that men might become enemies of the Cross of Christ by living in sin.

All the teaching of Scripture militates against this erroneous doctrine. It teaches us to balance the virtue of hope with a holy fear of the Lord so that the one will serve as a corrective for the other. It likewise commands us to give proof of our faith by the performance of good works. How can sinners be so misguided as to think that merely by trusting in the passion and death of Christ, without performing the works of virtue, they can be saved?

This should suffice to convince us of the necessity and blessings of the theological virtue of hope. And while there are many causes and foundations for supernatural hope, such as the goodness and mercy of God and the merits of the passion and death of Christ, we should likewise be mindful of God's divine providence. The realization that God exercises a fatherly care over us is sufficient to arouse in us a filial trust. Therefore, in all our works and trials we should confidently entrust ourselves to him. He is our Father and we can go to him and commend ourselves to him with the assurance that he loves us. He will never be deficient in giving us the help we need for our eternal salvation. This is what Jesus promised us: "What father among you will give his son a snake if he asks for a fish, or hand him a scorpion if he asks for an egg? If you, with all your sins, know how to give your children good things, how much more will the heavenly Father give the Holy Spirit to those who ask him" (Lk 11:10-13).

If God is with us, who can be against us? If he places us in his abundant pastures, what hunger or cold can ever afflict us? If he is the defender of our life, whom shall we fear? If he covers us with the shadow of his wings, who can harm us in any way?

Therefore, we may confidently say with David: "Even though I walk in the dark valley, I fear no evil; for you are at my side with your rod and your staff that give me courage.... The Lord is my light and my salvation; whom should I fear? The Lord is my life's refuge, of whom should I be afraid.... One thing I ask of the Lord; this I seek: to dwell in the house of the Lord all the days of my life, that I may gaze on the loveliness of the Lord and contemplate his temple" (Ps 23:4; 27:1, 4).

- 4 -

The Virtue of Charity

BEFORE WE TREAT OF THE PRACTICES and methods by which we may grow in the love of God, it will be well to consider the excellence of this love, for we are eager to undertake labors when the reward is great. And once we have received this precious jewel of charity, I do not doubt that we shall say with the spouse in the Song of Songs: "Deep waters cannot quench love, nor floods sweep it away" (Sg 8:7).

We cannot properly evaluate the worth of this virtue in a short chapter. Indeed, I do not know whether it would be better to honor it in silence, since it cannot be adequately praised with words. In fact, everything in Scripture or in the writings of the saints and mystics is either about charity or something that pertains to charity. Nevertheless, I shall point out very briefly the outstanding characteristics that place charity above all the other virtues.

In the first place, charity is the queen of all the virtues. To understand this, we should recall that the theological virtues of faith, hope and charity far surpass all the moral virtues, since they are concerned immediately with God as our supernatural end and they direct us to him, each in its own way. The virtue of faith sees God as First Truth and enables us to believe firmly all that God has revealed. The virtue of hope looks at God as our sovereign Good, whom we strive to attain with the help of his grace and our own meritorious good works. But charity embraces God as the supreme Good, who is worthy of being loved with the most intense love possible for what he is in himself.

By faith we see God obscurely and, as it were, beneath a veil. Hope looks to God as an arduous good not yet possessed but capable of being attained, and for this reason it carries with it a note of self-interest and a desire for our own perfection and happiness. But charity loves God with the love of authentic friendship, with a pure and disinterested love. As St. Bernard says, it does not seek its own interest.

The just soul possesses God through the virtue of charity because it is the nature of friendship love to fix all one's affections on the beloved, even to the extent of being transformed into the beloved. Thus, St. John says: "God is love, and he who abides in love abides in God and God in him" (1 Jn 4:16).

But if charity is the most excellent of all the virtues, the actual love of God is the best and most meritorious act that a man can perform. Nor is this contrary to the teaching on the excellence of martyrdom, because martyrdom is most pleasing to God precisely because of the charity behind it. Without charity, martyrdom would not even qualify as martyrdom in the strict theological sense.

The second excellence of charity is that it is not only the most noble of all the virtues; it is the very end and goal of all the divine commandments and counsels. They are all ordained to charity in one way or another. It is for this purpose that man has been fashioned by the hands of God.

The third excellence of charity is that it is not only the end and goal of all the other virtues, but it is the very soul and perfection of all the virtues. The body without the soul is still a body, but it does not have life; so also, without charity the virtues are still good habits but they do not have any life or merit before God. They can do nothing to make satisfaction for sin or to merit anything from God, though they may serve many other good purposes. St. Paul tells us: "If I have faith great enough to move mountains, but have not love, I am nothing. If I give everything I have to feed the poor and hand over my body to be burned, but have not love, I gain nothing" (1 Cor 13:2-3).

Charity alone is profitable and pleasing in the sight of God. In a way, charity can be compared to the Son of God, for just as no creature in heaven or on earth is pleasing to God except through Christ his Son, so no virtue or good work is pleasing to God unless it proceeds in some way from the virtue of charity. Our good works have no life or value unless they are informed and motivated by the virtue of charity.

However, if the Christian in the state of grace acts for the love of God, not only are his *good* deeds acceptable to God and meritorious, but even those works which are morally indifferent or purely natural. For that reason St. Augustine says: "Love and do what you will. If you are silent, you will be silent out of love; if you forgive, you will forgive out of love; if you punish, you will punish out of love; and whatever you do out of love is meritorious before God." Consequently, how greatly we should esteem that virtue which can make even the lowliest works meritorious in the eyes of God. Let us, therefore, heed the advice of St. Paul: "Whether you eat or drink — whatever you do — you should do all for the glory of God" (1 Cor 10:31).

The fourth excellence of charity is that it is not only the vital source of all the other Christian virtues, but it stimulates them, giving them the impulse to perform their various acts and functions. As St. Paul says, "The love of Christ impels us" (2 Cor 5:14). When the love of God is intense, it produces a fervent desire of pleasing him and of doing his holy will. Moreover, we know that nothing pleases God more than obedience, so the devout Christian strives to obey the divine commandments and to practice the virtues. This is the teaching of Christ: "Live on in my love. You will live in my love if you keep my commandments, even as I have kept my Father's commandments, and live in his love" (Jn 15:9-10).

"It seems to me," says St. Augustine, "that the briefest and most concise definition of virtue is to call it the proper order of love, for that is truly virtuous which gives all things their rightful share of love, loving them in the measure with which each one deserves to be loved, no more and no less.... Thus, charity is patient in adversity, temperate in prosperity, strong in times of passion, cheerful in the performance of good works, confident in times of temptation, liberal in hospitality, joyful among true brothers and patient among false brethren."

Even more inspiring are the words with which St. Paul praises the virtue of charity: "Love is patient; love is kind. Love is not jealous, it does not put on airs, it is not snobbish. Love is never rude, it is not self-seeking, it is not prone to anger; neither does it brood over injuries. Love does not rejoice in what is wrong but rejoices with the truth. There is no limit to love's forbearance, to its trust, its hope, its power to endure. Love never fails" (1 Cor 13:4-8).

Fifth, although charity is a great stimulus for all the virtues, it is especially so in regard to the virtue of fortitude. Charity undertakes great things, does not shy away from strenuous effort, is willing to confront great dangers, strengthens vacillating hearts and spurs us on to greater efforts, Charity does not measure difficulties by the rule of reason, but by the compass of our heart's desire. The reason for this is that the greater the love of the end or goal, the greater the impetus to strive to attain that goal. For that reason love readily takes great risks, even to the point of risking one's own safety for the defense of the beloved. The natural fear of danger to one's self is submerged by the fear of danger to the other.

Once again listen to the inspired words of St. Paul: "Who will separate us from the love of Christ? Trial, or distress, or persecution, or hunger, or nakedness, or danger, or the sword? As Scripture says: 'For your sake we are being slain all the day long; we are looked upon as sheep to be slaughtered.' Yet in all this we are more than conquerors because of him who has loved us" (Rm 8:35-36).

The sixth excellence of the virtue of charity is that it brings spiritual joy to the soul. When the Lord finds a person who seeks him and loves him truly, he inflames the will with the joy of the Holy Spirit, so that it can exclaim with David: "How lovely is your dwelling place, O Lord of hosts! My soul yearns and pines for the courts of the Lord. My heart and my flesh cry out for the living God" (Ps 84:4). This is clearly manifested in the lives of the saints, to whom the things of God were so sweet that they joyfully renounced all created things, sometimes even going into the solitude of the desert to live among the wild beasts of the wilderness. They could never have endured such a life but for the peace and consolation they received from God.

On the other hand, if men of science and research have dedicated themselves totally to their intellectual and scientific pursuits, it is not surprising that the devoted friends of God would dedicate themselves completely to the things of God. These souls are witnesses to the truth of Christ's words: "Come to me, all you who are weary and find life burdensome, and I will refresh you. Take my yoke upon your shoulders and learn from me, for I am gentle and humble of heart. Your souls will find rest, for my yoke is easy and my burden light" (Mt 11:28-30).

To conclude this discussion, let us observe that since charity is the greatest of all the virtues as well as the goal of all the others, the perfection of the Christian life must consist essentially in charity. Consequently, the perfection of holy souls, both in this life and in glory, is measured by the degree and intensity of their love. St. Bernard says that he who possesses great charity is great, but he who possesses little charity is little, and he who lacks charity is nothing. This is also the teaching of St. Paul, who said that if he has not charity, he is nothing (1 Cor 13:2).

If at the moment of death a person has a greater degree of charity than another person, he will receive a higher degree of glory in heaven than the other person. The reason for this is that one's eternal reward is measured by the intensity of one's love. St. Thomas Aquinas explains this by saying that the fact of having performed more good works or converted more souls does not of itself determine one's essential glory in heaven; the greater the *charity*, the greater the glory.

This is another way of saying, as St. Augustine did, that it is not the multitude of good works or the long years of service but the greater and more intense charity that determines greater merit and a greater reward. Nor should we be surprised at this, for although it is true that whatever we can do by ourselves is little in comparison with that which God gives us, we can nevertheless do much if we love much. In loving God as perfectly as we can, we are giving ourselves to him completely, and that is the greatest service we could possibly render to God. He who gives his love completely, gives all that he has and is. Such an offering is due only to God, but God reciprocates by giving himself in return.

This doctrine offers much consolation and encouragement to those who have little to give: those who, because of lack of education or ingenuity or because of sickness or old age, cannot perform great services and labor for the glory of God and the good of their neighbor. The person who loves much and gives himself totally out of love is already doing a great deal. Indeed, the desire to do much is already credited with doing much, because God reads our hearts, and in his eyes a good intention is of no less value than the work itself. If, therefore, you cannot do great deeds, then at least desire to do much and love as much as you can. In so doing, you will be doing great things for God.

You can judge from this how great is the excellence of the virtue of charity and how numerous are its benefits. Without charity, faith is dead, hope becomes a vain presumption, the merit of good works is lost, and the bond of fraternal love is destroyed. But with charity, we are strong in the face of all temptations, humble in all our works, and confident in the face of adversity.

- 5 -

The Perfection of Charity

IT IS THE COMMON TEACHING of the Church and all the saints that the perfection of the Christian life consists essentially in the perfection of the virtue of charity. St. Paul calls charity "the bond of perfection" (Col 3:14) and the goal of the law (1 Tm 1:5). The reason for this was explained by St. Thomas Aquinas: A thing is said to have reached its full perfection when it has attained the end or goal for which it was created, beyond which there is nothing else for which to strive. But the ultimate end of human existence, the purpose for which we were created, is to love the Lord our God with our whole heart and soul and mind and strength (Dt 6:5; Mt 22:37). Consequently, our spiritual perfection must consist in that which unites us to our supreme good and ultimate end. St. John tells us: "God is love, and he who abides in love abides in God, and God in him" (1 Jn 4:16). Therefore, the perfection of the Christian life consists primarily in the love that is charity.

But perhaps you will now ask what is the perfection of charity. St. Thomas Aquinas answers this question by saying that one may speak of the perfection of charity in three ways. The first and highest degree of the perfection of charity is to love God as much as he deserves to be loved. But only God can do that, since he alone has the infinite capacity for loving infinite goodness. The second perfection of charity is reserved for the souls in glory, who see the infinite beauty of God in

29

the beatific vision and will actually love him with all their heart and soul and mind and strength for all eternity. The third perfection of charity is that which is proper to this life, where one cannot yet attain to the perfection of love in glory, but can strive to love God to the best of one's ability (Mt 22:36-38). The perfection of charity in this life requires that one should strive to avoid sin, the proximate occasions of sin, and anything that would weaken the fervor of love. And since all the obstacles to the perfection of charity arise ultimately from self-love, one must wage a constant warfare against excessive self-centered love.

St. Augustine says that self-love can be controlled and lessened in this life but it can never be completely annihilated, because self-preservation is the first law of nature. He concludes that the perfection of charity in this life calls for a love that strongly resists and rejects anything that would weaken or prevent the actual love of God. This is the model that is given to us for the perfection of our love of God and we are commanded to strive for this degree of perfection in accordance with the precept given by Christ that we should love the Lord our God with all our heart and all our mind and all our strength. This precept, as we have said, cannot be fulfilled perfectly in this life, but what is possible in this life is to love God to the best of our ability and to renounce all worldly concerns and interests that are not required by our state of life or personal need. When a Christian has reached such a perfection of love in this life that he is detached from all perishable things and has no inordinate affection for any of them, so that his heart is habitually fixed on God, he will then be able to proclaim: "My lover belongs to me and I to him" (Sg 6:3).

I realize that few souls arrive at this degree of perfection and that the various duties of justice and charity frequently demand that we leave God for God. But we speak of this degree of perfection so that we may know the goal toward which we should travel as best we can. Even if many souls never reach such a lofty state in this life, they will approach it more closely if they direct their desires and intentions to greater things rather than to lesser things. Besides, Jesus addressed his words, "Be ye perfect," to all souls. In conformity with this teaching, we should always desire the best and greatest of good things; then perhaps we shall attain at least a portion of what we desire. A strong and intense desire takes no account of one's strength; it recognizes no limitations; it does not submit to the restrictions of reason. Lofty aspirations are not limited to what one *can* do, but what one desires to do.

But not every degree of charity suffices to give the peace and tranquillity of which we have spoken. Only perfect charity can give perfect peace and joy. When God so ordains, the soul can actually experience the goodness and sweetness of the Lord, as the Psalmist says: "Taste and see how good the Lord is" (Ps 34:9). As a matter of fact, we can enumerate eight degrees of charity through which the soul may pass until it ultimately reaches the state of perfect repose in God. These eight degrees of the perfection of charity are so closely linked to one another that the previous degree disposes for the one that follows.

The first degree is the *experiential knowledge* to which we have just referred. It is the gate through which the higher gifts and blessings of the Lord enter the soul and greatly enrich it. In the second degree the soul experiences *a strong impulse of love*. Since the virtue of charity operates through the human will, it bursts forth in love for the immense goodness of God that it has experienced. This is followed by *a most sweet delight*, a kind of hidden manna which is known only to the one who has tasted it. It is a normal effect of love and one of the principal means used by God to draw souls away from the world and detach them from all sensate pleasures. It so far surpasses every earthly satisfaction and delight that the soul readily renounces all lesser pleasures for it.

Since spiritual things are so excellent, the more they are tasted, the more they are desired. The mere taste produces a desire for more; so much so that the soul can find satisfaction in nothing else. Moreover, it realizes that it can enjoy spiritual goods only by self-denial and the practice of the virtues. Consequently, it experiences *an intense desire* not only to pray and meditate on spiritual truths but to imitate Christ and walk in his footsteps of humility, patience, obedience, self-denial, meekness and all the Christian virtues.

This desire is followed by *a sense of deep satisfaction*, for God does not arouse desires in us in order to torment us, but to perfect us and prepare us for even greater things. He it is who gives life and takes it away (Jb 1:21); he it is who arouses holy desires and satisfies those desires. Concomitantly he stirs up in the soul a great distaste for the things of this world, so that it can trample all earthly things underfoot. Once having tasted spiritual manna, the soul finds therein all pleasure and delight.

This leads to an experience which the mystics call *spiritual inebriation*, which far surpasses anything the soul has as yet experienced. At this stage the soul ignores all perishable goods and even passes beyond self and selfish interests; it is now submerged in the abyss of the infinite goodness and sweetness of God. The soul is now disposed for experiencing the seventh degree of charity, namely, *the assurance of salvation and eternal glory*. This assurance is not yet absolute, of course, because as long as we are in this life the most we can have is moral certitude. Hence, the prophet says: "Blessed is the man who trusts in the Lord, whose hope is the Lord" (Jr 17:7) and the Psalmist says: "I set the Lord ever before me; with him at my right hand I shall not be disturbed. Therefore my heart is glad and my soul rejoices, my body, too, abides in confidence; because you will not abandon my soul to the nether world" (Ps 16:8-10).

Last of all, this great confidence produces *a spiritual tran-*

quillity which is like a sweet sleep on the chest of the Lord. It is a peace that surpasses all understanding. This is the testimony of Isaiah: "My people will live in peaceful country, in secure dwellings and quiet resting places" (Is 32:18). This is the kingdom of heaven on earth and the paradise of delights that we are able to enjoy even in this earthly exile.

Certain souls, after having practiced prayer, mortification and works of charity, and after having walked along the path of the Lord with fervor of spirit and perseverance in the practice of virtue, ultimately reach that type of love which mystical theologians call "unitive love." Reaching this state is like reaching the promised land after traveling through the desert. Among the fruits of this love are a sweetness and joy that never cease, by day or by night. No matter what the activity, the soul cannot be separated from God. The sweetness of this love grips the devout soul and holds it captive, causing a strong distaste for the things of this world. God alone is the object of its desire; God alone is its treasure and its joy. All this is characteristic of unifying love.

He who reaches this union of divine love already enjoys in this life a happiness similar to that of glory. It brings a kind of plenitude, an interior repose and satisfaction that prompt the soul to repeat with St. Francis of Assisi: "O my God and my all! O my God and my all!" Nor is this a cause for surprise, for we were created for God, and once we are united with him, our souls are at rest. The clamor of all other desires ceases, for the soul then has no appetite for anything apart from God. Such is the happiness and contentment with which God rewards the works of his faithful servants even in this life.

After he had tasted the sweetness of this love, St. Augustine said: "The just man rejoices in you because your love is sweet and calm, and because you fill the hearts in which you dwell with sweetness, peace and tranquillity. Such things are not given by the love of the world or the flesh, which are distressing and filled with tribulation. They cannot bring peace

to the souls they enter; rather, worldly attachments bring sus-
picion, envy and many fears. But you, O Lord, are true delight for the good, for in you are found tremendous and over-
whelming tranquillity and a life that is alien to all anxiety."

In another place St. Augustine says: "What is this that I
experience? What fire is this that inflames my heart? What light
illumines it? O fire that ever burns and never dies, may I be
consumed by you! O light that ever shines and is never
eclipsed, illumine my soul.... O holy fire, how sweetly you
burn, how secretly you illumine, and how tenderly you inflame the soul!"

Moreover, charity not only makes a person enjoy peace
with God and one's neighbor, but also to be at peace with
oneself. It quiets the passions and eases the tension that arises
between the sensate faculties and the spirit. The internal warfare that we experience is a result of the struggle between the
flesh and the spirit, of the restlessness caused in us by our
inordinate desires. When the lower appetites are quieted, a
person can remain at peace, desiring nothing from this world
and even looking upon it with disdain.

Together with this internal peace, the Christian enjoys a
true liberty of spirit which is given to those who are no longer
slaves of their flesh. They reach a point where they enjoy the
liberty of the children of God, which enables them to gain a
mastery over all the passions that formerly ruled their lives.
The anxieties, worries and fears of this life do not disturb their
interior peace. They are so united to God that neither their
contacts with other people or their necessary duties and occupations can divert them from their awareness of the presence of God. Amidst a multitude of activities they preserve
their simplicity of spirit and they use all things as occasions
for raising their minds and hearts to God, for they can find
God in all things. In him is all their love and they remain so
absorbed in him that "seeing, they do not see, and hearing,
they do not hear."

What words can describe the virtues of these souls — the firmness of their faith, their confident hope, their joy in that which they love, their delight in the attainment of their holy desires, their peace in the midst of suffering, their undaunted courage in all their struggles? They experience delight in all their labors, wealth in their poverty, contentment in the midst of hunger, glory in times of persecution, honor in suffering, rest in their night vigils, and heavenly consolation in their practice of prayer.

The joys and delights of the love of God, who can expound them? He who wishes to know something of these things should meditate on the beautiful words of the Song of Songs: "Arise; my beloved, my beautiful one, and come! For see, the winter is past, the rains are over and gone. The flowers appear on the earth, the time of pruning the vines has come and the song of the dove is heard in our land. The fig tree puts forth its figs, and the vines, in bloom, give forth fragrance. Arise, my beloved, my beautiful one, and come! O my dove in the clefts of the rock, in the secret recesses of the cliff, let me see you, let me hear your voice, for your voice is sweet, and you are lovely" (Sg 2:10-14).

"O my soul," says St. Augustine, "much has the spouse of your soul given to you, but even more has he loved you.... Cast your eyes over this entire universe and see whether there is anything in it that is not for your service. All created nature was made for this purpose: to serve for your benefit and to contribute to your perfection. And who has arranged all this? To be sure, it was God himself. And how is it that you can accept all these benefits and not know the giver? What great folly it is not to desire the love of the omnipotent Lord! What great ignorance it is not to love him who loves you with an infinite love. Love him for what he is and love yourself and your neighbor out of love for him. Love him for yourself and love yourself for him."

But perhaps you will say that while it is true that the Lord is the spouse of souls, there are so many souls that he can give only a little love to each one. This may be true of human beings, who are limited in love, as they are in all the virtues, but the Lord is omnipotent in virtue and also in love. Consequently, no matter how many receive his love, there will never be a limit or terminus to his love. Just as no man receives less of the sun's rays than another, though the sun shines on all, so the Lord offers no less love to the countless souls of devout Christians than if there were only one holy soul to receive his love. God is not like Jacob, who loved Lia less because of his greater love for Rachel. Therefore, let others love what they wish, but I know for certain that all is well spent, even life itself, if at last I can be the recipient of his divine love.

- 6 -

The Gift of Wisdom

THE FUNCTION OF GRACE IS TO MAKE a person justified and pleasing in the sight of God. This cannot be achieved unless a person loves God, is sorry for sins committed in the past, and is sufficiently detached from the things of this world. But one cannot perform these acts unless he has sufficient knowledge, because the will is a blind faculty and cannot issue its command until the intellect first shows the way.

Moreover, St. Thomas Aquinas teaches that once the soul is justified, as it advances in the love of God, it also advances in the knowledge of divine goodness and beauty. Thus, if a person's actual love of God increases by one hundred degrees, his spiritual understanding should also grow in the same proportion. A person who loves much likewise knows the many reasons for loving, but one who loves but little will know but few reasons for loving.

If, as we believe, God dwells in the just soul through sanctifying grace, and if, as St. John points out, God is the light that illumines every man who comes into the world (Jn 1:9), then it follows that the more he finds the soul cleansed of sin and earthly attachments, the more resplendent will be the rays of his divine light in the soul. Similarly, the rays of the sun are more clearly reflected in a mirror that is clean and well polished. For that reason, St. Augustine calls God the wisdom of the purified soul. He wondrously illumines such a soul with the rays of his light and teaches it all it needs to know in reference to its eternal salvation.

But why should it seem so remarkable that God should do this for man, when he does something similar for all his creatures? The animals know by an instinct implanted in them by their Creator whatever they need to know for their self-preservation, both as individuals and as a species. Who taught the sheep which plants in the pasture are harmful and which are beneficial, so that they will instinctively eat the one and avoid the other? Who told them which animals are their friends and which are their enemies, so that they will follow the sheep-dog but flee from the wolf? It is the Creator who does these things, and if he gives animals the knowledge necessary for their preservation and well-being, how much more readily will he provide human beings with the knowledge necessary for the preservation of their spiritual life. If God has been so solicitous in providing for the natural order of things, how much more will he provide for things of the supernatural order, which are much more excellent but equally necessary for man's spiritual life.

Our own daily experience shows that there is such a knowledge as that of which we have spoken; it also reveals something about the type of this knowledge. It is not merely a speculative knowledge, given to us that we may simply know; it is a practical knowledge, so that we may act in accordance with that knowledge. The knowledge of spiritual truths is not given in order to form scholars who can discuss theology but to form virtuous Christians. Theological knowledge should not lie dormant in the intellect, as often happens with the learning acquired in the schools; it should enlighten and stimulate the will to perform the acts of virtue that foster our spiritual life.

Actually, this is the work of the Holy Spirit, who is the authentic teacher and guide of the spiritual life. He teaches his own what it is necessary for them to know, as Jesus promised: "When he comes, however, being the Spirit of truth, he will guide you to all truth" (Jn 16:13). In conjunction with this, we read in the Song of Songs: "I grew faint when he spoke" (Sg 5:6). These words show the great difference between this knowledge and other types of knowledge. The others do no more than inform the intellect, but the knowledge that comes through the Holy Spirit moves the will to do all that is necessary for the soul's conversion and growth in holiness. So we read in the Letter to the Hebrews: "Indeed, God's word is living and effective, sharper than any two-edged sword. It penetrates and divides soul and spirit, joints and marrow; it judges the thoughts and reflections of the heart" (Heb 4:12).

In other words, this spiritual knowledge makes a division between the animal and the spiritual parts of man and separates one from the other. In so doing, it liberates the spirit from the slavery that results from excessive attachment of the spirit to things of the flesh. And lest you think that this is an arbitrary teaching, listen to the words of the Psalmist: "I have more understanding than all my teachers when your decrees are my meditation. I have more discernment than the elders, because I observe your precepts" (Ps 118:99-100).

Hear also the promise made by God through the mouth of the prophet Isaiah: "Then the Lord will guide you always and give you plenty even on the parched land.... He will renew your strength, and you shall be like a watered garden, like a spring whose water never fails" (Is 58:11).

And what is the "plenty" with which God fills the souls of the just but the knowledge that he gives them concerning the truths of faith? He will teach them how great is the beauty of virtue; the ugliness of vice; the vanity of this world; the dignity of sanctifying grace; the splendor of heavenly glory; the sweetness of consolation from the Holy Spirit; the infinite goodness of God; the malice of evil and the shortness of this life. Isaiah tells us that by means of this knowledge, God frequently raises souls high above the mountains, where they contemplate the King in all his splendor, while their eyes see this present world as something remote and far away. Such blessings are a foretaste of the joys of heaven, which seems very near. But for those who reach out to clutch the things of earth, the joys of heaven are far distant or non-existent.

This is the reason why those who experience the gift of heavenly wisdom are neither puffed up in the days of their prosperity nor dejected in the time of adversity. Through the gift of wisdom they realize how insignificant are all the things that the world can give or take away when compared to that which God gives to the soul. So we read in the Book of Sirach: "Ever wise are the discourses of the devout, but the godless man, like the moon, is inconstant" (Si 27:12).

Commenting on these words, St. Ambrose says: "The wise man is not broken by fear; he does not change on gaining power; he does not become proud in times of prosperity; he is not deflated in times of adversity. For where there is wisdom, there is also virtue, constancy and fortitude." Consequently, the just man is always the same; he does not fluctuate with the changes that occur in his life nor does he follow every new doctrine. He remains faithful to Christ, established in charity and firmly rooted in faith.

We should not marvel that wisdom should have such great power. We have already stated that it is not a wisdom acquired in this world, but a heavenly wisdom; not a wisdom that inflates with pride, but one that edifies. It is not a wisdom that merely enlightens the intellect in a speculative way, but one that moves the will as it moved the will of St. Augustine, of whom it is written that he wept when he heard the psalms chanted in church. The voices of the chanters penetrated to the very depths of his heart and aroused such an intense devotion that tears streamed from his eyes.

O blessed tears and blessed wisdom that produced such wonderful fruit! What can be compared to such wisdom? We should not want to trade it for all the gold or silver in the whole world. The most precious gems could never equal it in value. This wisdom should arouse in you such a holy fear of God that you will abandon all your sinful ways. Although all that we have said about this heavenly wisdom is undoubtedly true, no man, however holy, should fail to subject himself in all humility to the direction and judgment of his superiors, especially to those who hold offices of dignity and authority in the Church. For who was more endowed with this heavenly wisdom than St. Paul, who had spoken to God, as it were, face to face? Yet he went to Jerusalem to communicate to the other apostles what he had learned in his remarkable vision "to make sure that the course I was pursuing, or had pursued, was not useless" (Gal 2:2). This shows that the internal assistance of grace does not exclude the external guidance of the Church. Divine providence makes use of both in order to supply for our deficiencies. But he who does not follow in all humility and docility the teaching and guidance of the Church, does not deserve the interior guidance and movements of grace.

- 7 -

The Path to Holiness

H AVING SPOKEN OF THE EXCELLENCE of charity and the gift of wisdom that perfects the virtue of charity, we shall now point out the pathway to the perfect love of God. But first we must understand clearly the goal that is sought. We have already explained that the supernatural virtue of charity unites the just soul to God in such a way that it is capable of sharing the selfsame desires and aversions of God himself. The reason for this is that the soul in the state of sanctifying grace shares in the life and holiness of God himself. The Lord asked this of us when he said: "Be holy, for I, the Lord, your God, am holy" (Lv 19:2).

One can readily deduce from this what steps are necessary to reach the goal of holiness, which connotes the most perfect possible imitation of God by a just soul. Now, a thing cannot become what it is not, unless it first ceases to be what it is. Consequently, the first requirement for attaining holiness is to "lay aside your former way of life and the old self which deteriorates through illusion and desire, and acquire a fresh, spiritual way of thinking. You must put on that new man created in God's image, whose justice and holiness are born of truth" (Eph 4:22-24). Hence, a man cannot become divinized unless he first cease to be human; that is, unless he first rise above the imperfection and weakness of his human nature. A person cannot become wise unless he first cease to be ignorant; he cannot be healthy until is he cured of his sickness or infection. In like manner, the Christian cannot become just and holy if he does not turn away from his sinful life.

There are two terms in every movement: that from which the mover departs and that toward which the mover travels, and it is not possible to arrive at the one without departing from the other. This is what some have called "the principle of reality," and it is based on the simple fact that we cannot be in two distinct places at the same time. As regards spiritual movement and progress in the spiritual life, the Christian must travel from self to God; he cannot attain to union with God unless he first departs from self.

Fire cannot ignite a piece of wood until the dampness has been driven out, because dampness is contrary to the heat of fire and the two cannot co-exist in the wood at the same time. Neither can man, conceived in original sin and clothed in flesh and blood, successfully be transformed into the sanctity of God unless he first lose all those characteristics and qualities that are incompatible with or contrary to the divine holiness. The transformation is eventually effected through the infusion of sanctifying grace, which is like a consuming fire that burns away the effects of sin and purifies the soul.

But St. Augustine has stated that God, who created man without man's help, will not save him or sanctify him without his help. We must cooperate with God by doing that which God has assigned to us, and our first task is to mortify ourselves and rid ourselves of any obstacle or impediment to our total transformation in God.

To plant a garden on a rocky terrain it is necessary to remove the rocks and clear away the weeds. Once this is done, the seeds can be sown or the seedlings planted. The same thing applies to the Christian life. One must work energetically to root out the weeds and briars of sin and evil inclinations. Once this has been done, one can proceed to plant the virtues, and especially the virtue of charity, which will grow into a tree of life in one's personal garden of Eden.

Accordingly, Cassian and other theologians taught that purity of heart is one of the most essential predispositions for the practice of the love of God. And purity of heart is acquired by uprooting from the heart everything and anything that could be an obstacle to the love of God. Therefore, the first thing required is the mortification of excessive self-love. Next, the devout Christian must be vigilant in observing the following practices: submission of his own will through faith and obedience; avoidance of sin and the proximate occasions of sin; prudent control of the emotions; restriction of involvement in worldly affairs; and daily examination of conscience.

Once the Christian is sufficiently mortified, that is, once he subjects his lower powers and faculties to reason and reason is guided by faith, the Holy Spirit can rule in him to such an extent that he is always disposed to approach God in love. It is also worth noting that any difficulty in the practice of the love of God is not caused by the exercise of love itself, which usually produces great sweetness and joy in the soul. Rather, the difficulty lies in ridding ourselves of the impediments to love. In other words, we encounter great resistance to the fire of love because our souls are so cold and damp. But once we have been warmed by holy desire, the fire of charity can burst into flame and will burn brightly.

A very important conclusion follows from this doctrine and it should help us avoid any misunderstanding concerning the pathway to holiness. We should not measure our progress in holiness by the sweetness or consolation that we may sometimes experience. Although these things are good in themselves, it is always safer and more accurate to measure our progress in terms of victory over the obstacles to holiness, our practice of self-denial, and strict control over self-centered love and the passions that flow from it.

Some individuals are so tender-hearted that the mere thought of the passion and suffering of Christ or something similar will immediately reduce them to tears and arouse them to great sympathy and compassion. But this frequently proceeds from a natural tenderness of heart rather than the pure love of God. Therefore, such persons should not think that they are making great progress in the spiritual life, unless the consoling experience is accompanied by a greater victory over their own self-will, their passions and evil inclinations.

- 8 -

The War Against Self-love

I N THE STATE OF INNOCENCE in which God placed man and woman at creation, nothing was more natural or more pleasant for them than to love God, their Creator. Unfortunately, original sin so severely wounded our integrated human nature that it could no longer practice the virtues with the joy and facility it formerly enjoyed. Instead, he who before his sin had loved God more than himself, afterwards was inclined to love himself more than God, But self-love is the primary obstacle to the love of God. It draws us into ourselves and away from God; it prompts us to love everything with a self-centered love. Consequently, anyone who truly desires to grow in the love of God must wage continual war against inordinate self-love. I say "inordinate" because if the love of oneself is regulated and controlled, it is not evil, but good and necessary. In fact, the first law of nature is self-preservation.

There are countless created goods that may stimulate selfish desires, but they can be listed under three distinct headings: money, honor and sensate pleasure. Thus, we read in St. John: "Have no love for the world, nor the things that the world affords. If anyone loves the world, the Father's love has no place in him, for nothing that the world affords comes from the Father. Carnal allurements, enticements for the eye, the life of empty show — all these are from the world. And the world with its seductions is passing away but the man who does God's will endures forever" (1 Jn 2:15-17).

The servant of God who understands this truth will take up his weapons and gird himself for battle against himself, marching under the royal banner of him who said: "If a man wishes to come after me, he must deny his very self, take up his cross, and begin to follow in my footsteps" (Mt 16:24). And if you want to know what this cross is, it is described by St. Paul: "Those who belong to Christ Jesus have crucified their flesh with its passions and desires" (Gal 5:24). In other words, Christian self-denial requires the repression of all one's evil inclinations and self-will so far as they are contrary to the will of God. A Christian may not be a law unto himself; he must obey the law of God.

The core of the Christian religion is the love of God and obedience to his laws as a proof of one's love. Love and obedience are closely related to each other, as Jesus said: "He who obeys the commandments he has from me is the man who loves me" (Jn 14:21). Therefore, prompt obedience should be a characteristic of the servant and friend of God. Spiritual writers call this "resignation" or "self-abnegation." It is called resignation because perfect obedience calls for the submission of our will to the will of God; it is called self-abnegation because perfect obedience to God's will requires that we mortify our own self-will.

There is nothing we can offer to God that is more pleasing to him than the resignation of our own will, because there is nothing we treasure more than our freedom of will. When we deny ourselves, even in small things, we can be sure that we have given to God a most acceptable service. If, for example, a person at table is offered an especially tasty dish that he could enjoy without any qualms, but he passes it up out of love of God and in imitation of Christ crucified, he is performing a work of virtue that is highly meritorious and pleasing to God. And if that is true in regard to small acts of self-denial, what must be the reward due to those who are resigned to God in all things, great and small? It is a great help in conquering self-love if we deny ourselves from time to time even in those things that are lawful. St. Paul gives us this teaching: "'Everything is lawful for me' — but that does not mean that everything is good for me. 'Everything is lawful for me' — but I will not let myself be enslaved by anything" (1 Cor 6:12). The same thing applies to all adversities, afflictions and trials. In all things we should conform to the divine will, placing ourselves in God's hands and always ready to accept the cross that he offers us. This is the way the saints and devout Christians gave up their own wills and subjected themselves to God. And if we want to practice this successfully, we should frequently say: "For love of you, my God, I refrain from seeing, hearing or tasting this or that; I deny myself this or that comfort or pleasure." In doing so, the Christian will gain much merit and will also make great progress in the virtues of love and obedience.

Self-love is difficult to control because it enters into almost every work that we perform. Similarly, self-will is so pervasive that frequently we do not even recognize or admit it. Sometimes it wears the mask of prudence, charity, or justice; at other times it may operate under an apparently good motive, such as making people do what is good for them or promoting some particular devotion. In all cases, however, self-will finds a way for the individual to do what he wants to do and avoid anything he is reluctant to do. All it needs is an apparently reasonable explanation.

The result is that such a person does his own will rather than God's will, although he may be completely unaware of doing so. In fact, he may believe quite the contrary. I would not say that such an individual is guilty of sin in each and every instance, but it is certainly true that he has been tricked into doing his own will under the guise of doing God's will. This is one of the reasons why it is so much better to be governed by the will of another than by our own will. The humble and docile subjection of obedience is a much safer path than the free choice of our own will. In any case we should be extremely cautious of desiring or committing ourselves to anything of importance until we have first examined it from every angle.

This is the way a Christian can arrive at the mortification of his own will, and once he has achieved this, he will understand the words of St. Paul: "After all, you have died! Your life is hidden now with Christ in God" (1 Col 3:3). And if you want to know when does a Christian arrive at the state of being dead to all things, I tell you that it is when he has abandoned his own will for God's will; when he has rid himself of inordinate self-love; when he has renounced worldly pleasures and satisfactions; when he does not burden himself with useless cares; when he does not sit in judgment on others; when he is not delighted with praise or saddened by criticism; when he suffers adversities patiently. Any Christian who lives this way is truly dead to self and alive in Christ.

- 9 -

Prayer and Recollection

YET ANOTHER MEANS FOR GROWING in the love of God is the practice of prayer and recollection. The necessity of this practice can be seen from the following example. If a woman wishes to preserve fruit that is somewhat sour and has a high acid content, she first cooks it until it loses the acidity and bitterness. Once this has been done, she adds sugar or syrup so that the fruit will absorb the sweetness of these condiments.

In like manner, if a man is to be transformed by the love of God, he must first rid himself of everything that is incompatible with the love of God. Once this has been done, he must then unite himself to God through the practice of prayer and recollection in order to be permeated with the spirit of the Lord.

The servant of God must exert every effort to proceed always with the divine assistance that is obtained through love and the practice of prayer. The Christian who perseveres faithfully in prayer and recollection will eventually be as beautiful as a cloud at sunset that is bathed in the rays of the setting sun.

This doctrine is based on two principles of philosophy, one of which states that causes have a natural tendency to produce effects that are similar to themselves, as happens when the cold winds cause other things to be cold or the sun's rays cause other things to radiate heat. The more powerful the cause, the more easily it reproduces itself in its effects.

The second philosophical principle states that causes in the natural order cannot produce their effects unless they are brought into contact with the material through which they produce their effects. Thus, fire cannot ignite wood unless it comes in contact with the wood and, indeed, unless the wood is properly disposed.

Now God is the first and most excellent and most powerful of all causes. He is also the most communicative and can produce the divine likeness in the souls of the faithful. To do so, however, the soul of the individual Christian must be properly disposed for intimate contact with God. And this union with God is not effected through man's approach to God by bodily steps; it is a spiritual journey in which man's rational faculties of intellect and will are united to God through sanctifying grace, charity and the practice of prayer.

St. Bernard speaks of four basic grades of prayer and recollection: spiritual reading, meditation, vocal prayer and contemplation. Spiritual reading walks; meditation runs; vocal prayer flies; but contemplation reaches the end of the journey and rests in God.

The Carthusian monk, Guigo II, had a similar listing: "Reading is an exercise of the external senses; meditation is concerned with the interior understanding; prayer proceeds from desire; contemplation outstrips every faculty. The first degree is proper to beginners; the second to advanced souls; the third to devout souls; the fourth to the blessed.... Reading without meditation is sterile; meditation without reading is liable to error; prayer without meditation is lukewarm; meditation without prayer is unfruitful; prayer, when it is fervent, wins contemplation, but to obtain contemplation without prayer would be rare, even miraculous."

The most beneficial type of spiritual reading is that which treats of the love of God and stimulates holy desires, as we find in the works of St. Augustine, St. Bernard and St.

Bonaventure. The best meditation is that which treats of the divine goodness and perfections, because this prompts one to the practice of virtue and the love of God. The most fruitful vocal prayers are those in which we ask for an increase of grace and virtue, especially if the prayers are inspired by an intense desire to grow in the love of God.

Speaking of those who are habitually occupied in the practice of prayer and recollection, St. Augustine says: "Blessed are they, O Lord, for whom you alone are the object of their hope and whose life is a perpetual prayer." It is indeed a great thing to be constantly recollected and it is not as difficult as some people imagine. We do not mean that one is always thinking about or talking to God. That, indeed, would be impossible, considering the numerous activities that call for our attention. What we mean by constant prayer is to preserve a recollected and vigilant heart, a holy fear and reverence for God, and a continual desire to please God and walk in his presence. In fact, this practice is very common with those who are truly dedicated to the love and service of God, whatever their state of life.

It goes without saying, of course, that of all the methods for walking in the presence of God, the best is the practice of actually loving God. Indeed, the act of loving is the proper exercise of the virtue of charity, and that is what constitutes the very essence of the perfection of the Christian life.

Any habit that is acquired by our own efforts will be strengthened and more deeply rooted in our personality by the repetition of acts. The supernatural virtues that are infused in our souls together with sanctifying grace will also be strengthened by the repeated acts of virtue. More than that, since they are supernatural powers, they are also the means by which we can merit an increase in grace and charity. St. Augustine said: "God gives us the grace to love him, and when we do, he gives us the grace to love him more." There are many ways in which the faithful soul can grow in holiness but the most direct and effective way is to raise our hearts to

God, to walk in his presence, making acts of love. This practice leads to true wisdom and mystical theology, which are not attained by reading and study but by praying and by raising our hearts to God in order to experience his goodness and appreciate the many graces and blessings that come from his love. "Taste and see how good the Lord is" (Ps 34:9).

The path that leads to this wisdom and mystical experience is to converse with God day and night. Although the duties of this present life sometimes make it necessary to be involved in earthly affairs, the spirit of God that dwells in our hearts brings us back to the things of heaven as soon as possible. Accordingly, if the servant of God wishes to be a disciple of heavenly wisdom, he should construct an oratory in his heart where he can always be recollected. I mean by this that he should walk always in the presence of God and conduct himself in all his affairs as if God were always at his side. Then he will never lose entirely the spirit of recollection or the devotion that flows from it. Scripture says: "I set the Lord ever before me; with him at my right hand I shall not be disturbed" (Ps 16:8).

This is what the servant of God should do, not with violence and force, however, but with calmness and peace, lovingly submitting his will to the sovereign Lord. And when he sees that he is easily distracted or disturbed, he should not be distressed; rather, he should gently try to return as soon as possible to his former state of recollection. And it is important to remember that we cannot achieve this by ourselves alone; we need God's help, but God never fails one who perseveres in doing all that he can.

God is present to all things that he has created, but he is especially present to the soul in the state of grace, because through sanctifying grace we share in the very nature and life of God himself. Hence, the Christian should work out his salvation in reverence, humility and holy fear. repeating to himself: "The Lord, in whose sight I stand, is present within me." Words such as these will help the devout soul return more quickly to an awareness of the presence of God when momentarily distracted by other activities. It is truly a cause for rejoicing to be able to live in the presence of God.

Blessed is the man who is never completely distracted from the divine presence by the company of other persons or the performance of any task. This is the state and condition of those souls who are so intimately united to God in love that the words of St. Paul apply to them: "Do you not know that you are the temple of God, and that the Spirit of God dwells in you?" (1 Cor 3:16). The soul is, as it were, hidden in God and so united with him through love that it cannot at the same time be intimately united to any created thing.

Having demonstrated that a principal means for growth in the love of God is the practice of constant prayer and the exercise of loving, we shall now treat of those things which are especially helpful in fostering these two practices. The first is to assign to ourselves one or two periods of silence during the day when we can be recollected in God so that we can turn our attention to the prayer and meditation we have already proposed for arousing the love of God in our hearts. If we are faithful to this practice, we shall more easily preserve a spirit of recollection throughout the rest of the day, and in due time the practice itself will be a source of such consolation and encouragement that we shall return to it whenever we can. But it should be noted that in these periods of recollection we should exercise control over the intellect, lest it become so speculative and analytical that the affections and movements of the will are impeded. At this time we should not be as concerned with knowledge and speculation about God as with the love of God. Therefore, we should loosen the reins on our will and put a brake on our intellect, allowing it only as much theorizing and speculative knowledge as is necessary for the enlightenment and guidance of the will. Then the will can extend its arms, as it were, to embrace God in the union of love.

These words of caution are very important because those

who do not follow this advice may end up using this exercise as a preparation for preaching or teaching instead of increasing their love of God. True, the intellect is the door through which truths enter and stimulate the will, but it sometimes happens that the truths are detained so long at the doorway of knowledge that they never reach the will. The result is that the intellect may be filled with new knowledge, but the will is empty and dry, so that the entire person remains empty and unsatisfied.

In order to understand how much better it is to love God than to know about him, listen to the words of Pico della Mirandola (+1494; brought back to orthodoxy by Savonarola): "Observe, my friend, what great foolishness is ours. When we consider the various faculties we have for uniting ourselves to God and enjoying his presence, we discover that we are able to love a great deal more than we are able to know. Therefore, by loving God we gain much more profit, and with much less effort. At the same time, whatever works we perform are thereby more acceptable to God. In spite of this, we are so foolish that we spend a great deal of time and effort in study, preferring to seek God through knowledge, without ever being able really to find him, rather than seek him through love. Indeed, if we do not love him, we shall not find him, and it will be our own fault."

If against this doctrine you assert that St. Thomas Aquinas teaches that the happiness of the blessed in heaven consists essentially in the knowledge of God and that therefore it is better to know God than to love him, I respond: In heaven we shall see God as he is in himself and this will suffice to make us perfectly happy for all eternity. In this life, however, we cannot see God as he really is, in all his glory and divine beauty, but only in proportion to our limited capacity and according to our human mode of knowledge and understanding, which is very small indeed. Similarly, the Atlantic Ocean cannot enter the straits of Gibraltar in all its immensity, but only in the measure that the straits can receive the ocean. So in this earthly life we know and understand God by making him fit into our human mode of understanding. Hence St. Paul says: "At present we see indistinctly, as in a mirror, but then face to face. At present I know partially; then I shall know fully, as I am fully known" (1 Cor 13:12).

But the love of God does not work in that way. Love transforms the lover into the object that is loved, so that the lover becomes one thing with the beloved. Once more we can see the vast difference between knowing God and loving him. In this life we know God as best we can, so far as our finite minds permit, but we are able to love him as he is in himself. In other words, in knowing God we make him fit into the categories of our limited human intellect, but in loving him we are made to his measure by being transformed into him through love.

For the same reason the philosophers tell us that it is better to love lofty and divine things than simply to know them, but it is better to know lower and inferior things than to love them. In knowing inferior things we spiritualize them, so to speak, by making them intellectual and proportionate to our human intellects, but in loving them we lower ourselves because the object of our love draws us to itself. On the other hand, the knowledge of lofty and divine things does not make them more excellent; it lessens them, in a way, by adapting them to our human intellect so that we may know them. But when we love lofty things, this does not happen, because in loving them we do not change those things into ourselves; rather, we are somehow changed into them. If we love good things, we ourselves become good; if we love evil, we become evil, for a man becomes what he loves. Once more we see how important it is for the Christian to strive energetically to love God above all things with all his heart and soul and mind and strength.

In order that the practice of the love of God may be constant and fruitful, one must be motivated by a vehement desire. And to stimulate such a desire, it suffices to consider the countless blessings that God has showered upon us and the consolation and sweetness that come from tasting the goodness of the Lord. The following example may help to demonstrate the vehemence of this holy desire. If a woman has lost a precious jewel of great value to her, she can't eat or sleep until she finds it, and if she does eat, she pays no attention to what she is eating. Neither does she care to converse or associate with other people, because her mind is totally preoccupied with the lost jewel. But if the woman searches so intently for a gem of earthly value, with what greater persistence and anxiety should she seek the precious pearl of the spiritual life. A person who is impelled by this desire will search for God everywhere, and everything in life becomes another motive for loving God.

A person wearing colored glasses will see that everything is tinted in that color. In like manner, the Christian whose heart is permeated with the love of God will see and judge all things as somehow related to the object of his love. Indeed, everything serves as a motivation for greater love. Eventually the love becomes a raging fire that inflames everything it touches. Even the water thrown on the fire makes the flames burn more brightly.

The effort to be constantly loving God and ever desiring an increase of love, begging God in all humility and with deep devotion for the living flame of love, is the proper study of mystical theology. We are referring to the loving knowledge or awareness of God that is attained not so much by study and intellectual argumentation as by the affections and desires of the will. God will not fail to respond to such longings and desires, seeing that the soul is as sad and afflicted as another Magdalen in searching for him. He will call the soul and draw it after him in the odor of his ointments (Sg 1:3). For how is it possible that he would deny those who seek him, when he himself has given them the grace to seek him. He desires nothing more than to give himself to souls that long for divine love and union with God.

- 10 -

Call to Action

ONE OF THE GREATEST OBSTACLES to the love of God is the vice of sloth, which is a laziness or languor of spirit in regard to the performance of good works and the practice of virtue. Unless corrected, it can lead to a repugnance or distaste for spiritual things. It is a capital sin, and therefore it is the source of numerous other sins such as malice, rancor, pusillanimity, lack of self-confidence, attachment to vain and useless things, and a stubborn refusal to obey God's commandments. Christ warned against slothfulness in the following words: "Even now the ax is laid to the root of the tree. Every tree that is not fruitful will be cut down and thrown into the fire" (Mt 3:10). On another occasion, when admonishing his disciples to be vigilant, he said: "Stay awake, therefore! You cannot know the day your Lord is coming" (Mt 24:42).

All Christians can take to heart the words of St. Paul to Timothy: "I remind you to stir into flame the gift of God bestowed when my hands were laid on you. The Spirit God has given us is no cowardly spirit, but rather one that makes us strong, loving and wise.... With the strength which comes from God bear your share of the hardship which the gospel entails" (2 Tm 1:6-8).

Think of the many trials and labors that Christ endured for your sake, from the beginning until the end of his life. Think of how many nights he passed without sleep, praying for you;

how he traveled throughout Galilee preaching and healing the sick; how he was always working for your eternal salvation; how he carried the heavy weight of the cross on his shoulders, already lacerated and bleeding from the scourging at the pillar. If our Lord suffered so much to free you from the bondage of sin, could you not accept a little suffering in order to do penance for your past sins?

Consider also the labors and hardships endured by the apostles as they traveled throughout the known world proclaiming the good news of the gospel; the torments and pain suffered by the martyrs; the labors and vigils of confessors and virgins; the solitude and mortification of countless contemplatives who withdrew from the world to live in closer union with God. Think of the communion of saints, now reigning in heaven, who extended the kingdom of God throughout the world by their preaching, their works of charity, and the example of their holy lives.

In addition to this, think of the effort expended by merchants and businessmen to accumulate wealth and possessions that they cannot take with them. With what greater reason should you be concerned about eternity and work for heavenly treasures that will last forever. And remember that if you do not work now, when you have the time and the strength, later on you will live to regret your sloth and indifference. Life is short and filled with many anxieties, so make the most of the time, and work while you can. The night will come when you cannot work.

To make satisfaction for our numerous sins, it is necessary to do penance and also make a firm resolution to amend our lives. St. Peter denied Christ three times, and for the rest of his life he wept over his sin, although Jesus had already pardoned him. A sinful woman performed a penitential act by bathing the feet of Jesus with her tears and wiping them with her hair. She had the consolation of hearing him say: "Your sins are forgiven.... Your faith has been your salvation.

Now go in peace" (Lk 7:48-50). I shall not attempt to enumerate the other examples of penance and atonement for sin. I shall simply say that perhaps in many cases the sins of those penitents were much less serious than our own. Those people who daily add to the number of their sins should pause to consider the seriousness of their obligation to repent and to do penance. Now is the time of forgiveness, mercy and grace. By means of penitential acts and good works in this life we are able to merit the blessings of eternal happiness. Our works and efforts may seem small indeed, but if they proceed from grace and love, they are of great merit. Our good works are only temporal, but the reward for them is eternal. The time spent in running the race is brief, but the merited crown is everlasting. We should not let this time of merit pass by without profiting from it.

If at times we find that we are overwhelmed by many preoccupations and labors, let us remember the admonition of Scripture: "We must undergo many trials if we are to enter into the reign of God" (Ac 14:22). St. Paul told Timothy: "Bear hardship along with me as a good soldier of Christ Jesus" (2 Tm 2:3). And if you feel that you have already struggled and labored enough, remember the words of Christ: "If a man wishes to come after me, he must deny his very self, take up his cross, and begin to follow in my footsteps" (Mt 16:24).

Unless we persevere until the end, our efforts will not produce the desired results; there will be no reward for our labors; the runner in the race will not achieve victory. For that reason Christ did not come down from the cross when the Jews demanded; he did not want to leave the work of our redemption unfinished. And if we wish to be faithful imitators of Christ, we must work diligently until death. Let us never cease to do penance for our sins and to carry our cross in imitation of Christ. Otherwise, what shall it avail us if we have navigated the ocean of life and at the end we do not reach port?

Nor should we be dismayed at the difficulties we meet in our efforts and labors. God has promised us that if we struggle manfully, he will help us conquer. If we pray: "O God, come to my assistance; O Lord, make haste to help me," we can confidently hope that God will come to our aid when we are in need and will reward us when we are victorious, with the help of his grace. Therefore, when you are fatigued by your labors, do not compare the difficulty in the practice of virtue with the pleasure to be found in sin; rather, compare the temporary pleasure you may find in your sin with the everlasting joy that will be yours in heaven. These comparisons should help you admit that it is much better to follow the path of virtue than to choose vice.

   .   If perchance you lose a battle, do not become discouraged. It does sometimes happen that after a period of victory a person becomes careless and overconfident. To lose a battle does not mean that one has lost the war. But when a person does fail, it should prompt him to be even more vigilant in the future and to be prepared for the next battle when the trumpet sounds. Remember also that there is no ocean without waves and there is no Christian life without temptations. In fact, a person who begins to lead a good Christian life is usually more strongly tempted by the devil; he does not have to tempt those who are already under his power. Therefore you must be as ready and alert as if you were on the front lines of battle. And however severely you may be wounded in battle, do not surrender; rather, use it as an incentive to fight even more courageously.

   There is in fact a great deal to be gained from one's weakness and failure in battle. For one thing, it shows the combatant where he has failed to measure up and where he needs to strengthen himself against the enemy. Moreover, even if one is wounded time and again, he should realize that this is the lot of those who fight bravely. The courageous soldier is not necessarily the one who has never been wounded, but the one who has never surrendered. And a soldier is not conquered by suffering many wounds, but only if he loses his courage. If, therefore, you have been wounded in the struggle, tend the wound immediately, for it is much easier to heal a fresh wound than one that has become infected.

If in the warfare against the world, the flesh and the devil, you are sorely tempted, do not give in to the temptation but resist bravely. The very temptations we encounter can prompt us to be more assiduous in the practice of virtue. With the help of God's grace, you will never be any worse off for having been tempted; in fact; you will be better, because in resisting the temptation, you have made it a means for growth in virtue.

Hence, if you are tempted to gluttony or lust, put aside your usual comforts for a time, even those that are lawful, and increase your fasting and pious exercises. If you are tempted to avarice, increase your almsgiving and works of charity. If you are tempted to vanity, humble yourself and withdraw yourself from the attention of others. If you act this way, the devil will not dare to tempt you further; he doesn't want to give you an opportunity to deny yourself and practice virtue. Remember, the devil wants you to commit sin; so avoid slothfulness as much as possible. Never be so idle, even in your leisure time, that you cannot find something worthwhile to do; but never be so busy that you cannot in the midst of your duties occasionally raise your mind and heart to God.

- 11 -

Love of Neighbor

THE IMPORTANCE OF LOVE of neighbor and the frequency with which it is recommended in Sacred Scripture can be appreciated by anyone who has read the Bible. Both the Old Testament and the New Testament contain admonitions concerning the love of neighbor. In Isaiah, for example, we learn that the Jews complained, saying: "Why do we fast, and you do not see it; afflict ourselves, and you take no note of it?"

And God said: "Lo, on your fast day you carry out your own pursuits.... Yes, your fast ends in quarreling and fighting, striking with wicked claw.... Is this the manner of fasting I wish, of keeping a day of penance: that a man bow his head like a reed and lie in sackcloth and ashes? Do you call this a fast, a day acceptable to the Lord? This, rather, is the fasting that I wish: releasing those bound unjustly, untying the thongs of the yoke; setting free the oppressed, breaking every yoke; sharing your bread with the hungry, sheltering the oppressed and the homeless; clothing the naked when you see them, and not turning your back on your own.

"Then your light shall break forth like the dawn, and your wound shall quickly be healed; your vindication shall go before you, and the glory of the Lord shall be your rear guard. Then you shall call, and the Lord will answer; you shall cry for help, and he will say: Here I am" (Is 58:3-9).

You can see from this that God considers love of neighbor an essential part of true justice and he wants us to act in this way toward our neighbors. And what shall I say of the teaching of St. Paul? Is there any letter in which he does not highly recommend that we practice love of neighbor? How greatly he praises the virtue of charity and how minutely he describes its wonderful attributes. He tells us that it is the most excellent of all the virtues and is the most certain pathway to union with God.

Not content with this, he states in his Letter to the Colossians: "Over all these virtues put on love, which binds the rest together and makes them perfect" (Col 3:14). And in the Letter to the Romans he says: "He who loves his neighbor has fulfilled the law.... The commandments... are all summed up in this: 'You shall love your neighbor as yourself'" (Rm 13:8-9). What greater praise could be given to any virtue? What Christian, desirous of knowing the best way to please God, will not resolve to perform all his actions under the impetus of love?

In addition to these testimonies, we have the teaching of St. John the Evangelist, the beloved disciple. He repeats nothing more insistently than the doctrine on charity. And when he was asked why he constantly repeats the same teaching, he answered by saying that if the practice of charity were properly implemented, it would suffice for our salvation. This is true even if one's love seems cold and dry, because what matters is that love should produce its effects — the works that flow from charity. Otherwise it would not deserve the name of love. St. John tells us: "I ask you, how can God's love survive in a man who has enough of this world's goods yet closes his heart to his brother when he sees him in need? Little children, let us love in deed and in truth and not merely talk about it" (1 Jn 3:17).

Some persons say that they love but their love is only a word; they do not pass beyond that to perform the works of love. Others love and also help their neighbor with all kinds of free advice and good counsel, but they never open their purse to help the poor. Still others love and advise and help the needy according to their means, but they have no patience with the weaknesses and the annoyance of others. Consequently, for all their good works, they do not follow the teaching of St. Paul: "Love is patient; love is kind.... There is no limit to love's forbearance, to its trust, its hope, its power to endure" (1 Cor 13:4, 7).

Then there are others who can endure insults and injuries with great patience, but they cannot forgive and forget. They may have no hatred in their hearts, but they are unable to show a pleasant face. They strive in many ways to do all things well, but their expression is one of grim determination. And they really do succeed in doing all things well, but because of their attitude, they do not edify their neighbor by word and deed, as is required by true fraternal charity.

Each Christian can examine his or her conscience in regard to the things we have described, in order to see how much is present or lacking in their practice of fraternal charity. To summarize the degrees of perfection of love of neighbor, he who does no more than profess his love is in the first and lowest degree of fraternal charity; he who loves and gives counsel is in the second degree; he who actually helps his neighbor is in the third degree; he who patiently endures annoyances is in the fourth degree; he who endures and pardons is in the fifth degree; but one who does all these things and edifies others by his holy life has reached the apex of fraternal charity. This is the mark of a perfect and apostolic Christians.

There are also negative aspects of charity; namely, things we ought not do. For example, we should not judge others or speak ill of them; we should not do harm to them or their friends and possessions; we should not scandalize them by word or deed or be discourteous to them. The person who obeys these admonitions will be able to fulfill perfectly everything that is commanded by the precept of charity.

If you want to make progress in this area, try to cultivate the heart of a mother toward your neighbor. This is one sure way of fulfilling the precept of charity. Observe how a good mother loves her child; how she gives good advice when needed; how she supplies all the child's needs, puts up with his tantrums and selfishness with great patience, but reprimands and corrects when necessary. All her actions are prompted by charity, which is the queen of all the virtues. See how a good mother rejoices when a child behaves well but is saddened by his faults and misdeeds. On the other hand, she experiences the disappointments and sufferings of her child as if they were her own. Her deep concern for the welfare of her child prompts her to pray constantly for his well-being. She is more attentive to the needs of her child than she is to her own. She denies herself in so many ways so that she can be more generous to her child. Such is the way of a mother.

If you are able to cultivate this kind of attitude toward your neighbor, you will be well on the way to the perfection of fraternal charity. And if as yet you are unable to practice these things, then at least desire to do so. Make that the goal of your striving in dealing with your neighbor.

But, you may ask, how it is possible to have this kind of love for a stranger? I reply that you should not look upon your neighbor as a stranger, but as the image of God and a child of the heavenly Father. Your neighbor is as much the work of God's hand as you are. St. Paul reminds us that we are all members of Christ and that anyone who sins against his neighbor is likewise sinning against Christ. On the other hand, anyone who does good to one's neighbor is also doing good to Christ. Did not Christ identify himself with our neighbor when he said: "I assure you, as often as you did it for one of my least brothers, you did it for me" (Mt 25:40)? Consequently, you should not look at your neighbor merely as such and such a person, but as a member of the mystical body of Christ and a child of our Father in heaven.

Consider for a moment the bond of love that unites those who are related by flesh and blood. Are you not ashamed if sanctifying grace does not mean more to you than human relationships or if spiritual union with God is not more important to you than the union based on family ties? St. Paul reminds us that we Christians have one God and Father of all, one Lord, one baptism, one faith, one hope, and one Spirit that gives us life (Eph 4:4-6).

In other words, all Christians have God as their Father, the Church as their mother, Christ as their Lord, one faith as a supernatural light shared by all, firm hope in the one and the same pledge of glory, one baptism that makes us adopted children of the heavenly Father, one nourishment which is the Holy Eucharist, wherein we are united with Christ. In addition to all this, through sanctifying grace we all share in the same Holy Spirit, who dwells in the souls of the faithful to vivify and sustain them.

Finally, cast your gaze on Christ, who loves us so ardently, so tenderly, so steadfastly and unselfishly. Inspired by his example, let us love one another as he loved us. This was the commandment he left us at the Last Supper: "Love one another as I have loved you" (Jn 15:12).

- 12 -

The Moral Virtues

T HERE ARE TWO GENERAL classifications of virtues in the Christian life: the *theological virtues* of faith, hope and charity, and the *cardinal virtues* of prudence, justice, fortitude and temperance. Under these four headings we can list all the numerous *moral virtues*. The theological virtues relate to God himself as our ultimate end; the moral virtues relate to our human actions, which should serve as steps on our journey to heaven. Our morally good acts are the rungs on the ladder of perfection and are meritorious when performed in the state of grace.

The Virtue of Prudence

The virtue of prudence is to the spiritual life what the eyes are to the body, the captain is to a ship, the driver is to an automobile, for it guides the Christian on his way to perfection and salvation. Without this virtue, the Christian would be unable to make the right judgments and choices that proceed from a rightly formed conscience. That is why the holy abbot Antony named prudence as the master and guide of all the other virtues.

The functions of the virtue of prudence are numerous and diverse. It is one of the four "cardinal" virtues and is so called because it is a general virtue that intervenes in the acts of all the other virtues, including the theological virtues. In fact, the adjective "cardinal" comes from the Latin word *cardo*, meaning hinge, because there are numerous particular virtues that are related to or are parts of the four cardinal virtues. Presupposing the virtues of faith and charity, Christian prudence directs all our actions toward God as our ultimate end, carefully discerning whether a given action is motivated by love of God or love of self. Prudence also directs our actions toward our neighbors, so that we may help them and not scandalize them. Experience teaches, however, that we cannot avoid all the imperfections and weaknesses of human life, especially when we consider the effects of original sin. Moreover, Aristotle taught that we do not always have perfect certitude in all things, because some things can be clearly demonstrated but others not. So the prudent man does not expect perfection in every particular activity; to demand it in every circumstance may cause more harm than good.

In order to be sure of making prudent judgments and choices, one must know himself so well that he recognizes his good qualities as well as his evil inclinations and moral defects. Knowing and admitting these things, he will be able to exercise caution and vigilance, knowing when to draw back and when to go forward. In Sacred Scripture the Book of Sirach is filled with practical advice and admonitions for practicing the virtue of prudence.

Prudence enables us to approach our occupations and activities with a spirit of moderation so that we shall not be overwhelmed by too much work. St. Francis of Assisi says in his Rule that all things should serve for our spiritual improvement. Consequently, prudence prevents us from giving ourselves so completely to external works that we lose our peace of soul and neglect the practice of prayer and recollection. The apostles were well aware of this danger when they withdrew from certain activities and delegated others to take their place, saying: "This will permit us to concentrate on prayer and the ministry of the word" (Ac 6:4). No one should presume that he alone can do everything; in fact, he will accomplish little who attempts to do too much. By exercising prudence we can learn to ignore the opinions and judgments of worldly persons, whose conversation is nothing more than the yapping of dogs that never stop barking but have no reason to bark at all. St. Paul warns us: "Whom would you say I am trying to please at this point — men or God? Is this how I seek to ingratiate myself with men? If I were trying to win man's approval, I would surely not be serving Christ" (Gal 1:10). There is no greater folly than to be swayed by the opinion of the crowd.

Prudence is also necessary if we are to succeed in managing our affairs and avoid making mistakes that will have to be corrected later with great difficulty and inconvenience. This means that we should not rush headlong to the task we are to perform or the decision that has to be made. Serious or complex matters call for lengthy deliberation, and sometimes for seeking advice from others. First of all, as devout Christians we should commend our task to the Lord. Second, we should give much thought to the project at hand, considering not only the work itself but also the circumstances. Third, we should, when necessary, take counsel with other experienced persons, taking care that the persons are knowledgeable and carefully selected. Fourth, if time permits, it is often better to let the matter rest for a few days before making the final decision; it sometimes happens that after deliberation we find it necessary to judge differently.

There are four distinct impediments to the proper exercise of prudence: rashness, passion, obstinacy and pride. Rashness acts impetuously and without sufficient deliberation. Passion blinds the reason and impedes logical thinking. Obstinacy stubbornly clings to one's own opinion and makes one deaf to any further suggestions. Pride inflates a person with the vanity and pomposity that preclude any dialogue or collegiality.

Since prudence is, so to speak, the moral virtue *par excellence*, it is characterized essentially by that which is proper to any act of virtue, namely, that it avoids all extremes. It holds to the middle course, which the ancient philosophers called "the golden mean." Therefore, the prudent man does not condemn everything nor does he justify everything; he knows that universal judgments are frequently erroneous judgments. He is guided in all things by the rule of reason; he avoids prejudice; he tries to be objective in all his judgments and opinions.

Prudence does not consider the antiquity or the newness of things in order to make a favorable judgment about them. Some old things should be replaced; some should be venerated and preserved. The fact that something is ancient does not on that account mean it should be rejected, nor does the newness or novelty of a thing automatically mean it is better. Prudence looks first at the merits of things in themselves and does not judge solely by age or appearances. Vice gains nothing by being old except that it is more deeply rooted; virtue loses nothing by being new except that it is not yet proven. Aristotle says that sometimes a lie has more the appearance of truth than truth itself.

Gravity and deliberation are the hallmarks of the virtue of prudence. Consequently, the prudent man will not be too quick to believe, to concede, to promise, to judge, to carry on frivolous conversation or to react with emotion. These are the actions of an imprudent person. He who believes too readily shows levity of spirit; he who promises too quickly may commit himself to too much; he who concedes in haste may live to regret it; he who engages in idle conversation may be guilty of calumny or detraction; and he who quickly reacts with emotion shows that he is infantile and unstable. This virtue is the virtue that marks maturity, which is the fruit of experience.

Consequently, St. Thomas Aquinas taught that we cannot expect to find the virtue of prudence in children. Let us now consider how one can acquire and develop the virtue of prudence. One of the quickest and best methods is to learn from one's own experience and the experience of others. And to do this, one must have good powers of observation and a good memory. For that reason it is said that memory is a good teacher of prudence, and that our today is a student of our yesterdays. Hence, we read in Ecclesiastes: "What has been, that will be; what has been done, that will be done. Nothing is new under the sun. Even the things of which we say: 'See, this is new!' has already existed in the ages that preceded us" (Ec 1:9-10).

The virtue of prudence is greatly fostered by the virtue of humility; and conversely, it is most impeded by the vice of pride. "When pride comes, disgrace comes; but with the humble is wisdom" (Pr 11:2). Jesus proclaimed to his heavenly Father: "What you have hidden from the learned and the clever you have revealed to the merest children" (Mt 11:25). But humility should not be so extreme that a person concedes in everything or lets himself be influenced by every wind. That would not be humility but fickleness and even cowardice. True humility must be founded on truth. So we read in Scripture: "When invited by a man of influence, keep your distance.... Engage not freely in discussion with him, trust not his many words; for by prolonged talk he will test you, and though smiling he will probe you" (Si 13:9, 11).

Finally, devout prayer is also a great help for acquiring prudence, because one of the principal functions of the Holy Spirit is to enlighten our minds through the gifts of science, understanding, counsel and wisdom. The greater a person's humility and the more fervent his practice of prayer, the greater his docility in presenting himself to be instructed as a child of God.

The Virtue of Justice

The subject matter of the virtue of justice is specified in general under the first law of morality: Do good and avoid evil. This law is self-evident; as soon as an individual reaches the age of reason, he or she knows this law. Its application, however, must be learned by study and experience.

Under the first part of this precept — do good — we are commanded to practice the virtues; under the second part — avoid evil — we are commanded to avoid sins of all kinds. The practice of the virtue of justice obliges us to render what is due to God, to self, and to neighbor. The fulfillment of the obligations arising out of justice requires us to observe the proper balance between rights and duties; to go to extremes on either side would be a violation of justice. The Christian who is truly just will relate as a child toward God, as a brother or sister toward neighbor, and as a judge toward self. This is what the Lord requires of us; namely, that we exercise sound judgment in regard to ourselves, mercy toward our neighbor, and solicitude in the service of God.

Anyone who reads the Bible will soon learn the importance of observing the rules of justice in our relations with others, both toward God and toward our neighbor. Basically our duties toward God are fulfilled in our observance of the virtue of religion, which is one of the particular virtues listed under the cardinal virtue of justice. These duties are summarized in the first three commandments of the Decalogue: "I, the Lord, am your God.... You shall not have other gods besides me.... You shall not take the name of the Lord, your God, in vain.... Remember to keep holy the Sabbath day" (Ex 20:2, 7, 9). This revelation to Moses indicates that the practice of the virtue of religion, flowing from a belief in the existence of God, is an obligation for every human being.

As regards justice toward our neighbor, the Old Testament contains God's command that we practice justice in charity toward our fellow human beings. When the Jews asked God why they had fasted but he did not see it or take any account of it, he responded through the prophet Isaiah: "Lo, on your fast day you carry out your own pursuits, and drive all your laborers. Yes, your fast ends in quarreling and fighting, striking with wicked claw.... Do you call this a fast, a day acceptable to the Lord? This, rather, is the fasting that I wish: releasing those bound unjustly, untying the thongs of the yoke, setting free the oppressed, breaking every yoke; sharing your bread with the hungry, sheltering the oppressed and the homeless, clothing the naked when you see them, and not turning your back on your own" (Is 58:3-7).

Likewise, when Bethelsarezer sent men to ask the priests and prophets about the practice of abstaining and mourning in the fifth month, this word of the Lord came to Zechariah: "Thus says the Lord of hosts: Render true judgment, and show kindness and compassion toward each other. Do not oppress the widow or the orphan, the alien or the poor; do not plot evil against one another in your hearts" (Zc 7:8-10).

But perhaps nowhere in the Old Testament do we find a stronger warning to those who violate justice than in the words of God concerning Sodom: "Look at the guilt of your sister Sodom: she and her daughters were proud, sated with food, complacent in their prosperity, and they gave no help to the poor and needy. Rather, they became haughty and committed abominable crimes in my presence; then, as you have seen, I removed them.... For thus speaks the Lord God: I will deal with you according to what you have done, you who despised your oath, breaking a covenant" (Ezk 16:49-50, 59).

Turning to the New Testament, which contains the teaching on the virtue of charity, we find ample proof of the importance of the virtue of justice. Christ makes fraternal justice and charity the basis for the final judgment. He will judge each soul according to its performance of the works of mercy. What more needs to be added to his statements that if we have done these things for the least of his brethren, we have done it for him, and that the love of God and neighbor is the sum of the whole law? And in his sermon at the Last Supper he stressed most emphatically the love of neighbor and the works of charity performed for one's neighbor. This, he told us, is his commandment; that we love one another *as he loved us*. In other words, Christ's love for us, for whom he died, is the standard and measure of our love for our neighbor.

St. John, the beloved disciple, repeats nothing more frequently than the command that Christians should love one another. "Beloved, let us love one another," he says, "because love is of God; everyone who loves is begotten of God and has knowledge of God. The man without love has known nothing of God, for God is love" (1 Jn 4:7-8). This teaching on Christian fellowship in love is at the same time a verification of the Catholic teaching that the virtue of charity is the crown of all the virtues, including the virtue of justice.

The Virtue of Temperance

The very word "temperance" designates the human quality that should characterize the practice of the virtue of the same name; a temperate quality that is neither too ardent nor too cold. We conclude from this that the virtue of temperance does not exclude the enjoyment of legitimate sensate pleasure; it simply calls for moderation. By stipulating *moderation*, we are stating something that is required for each and every act of every virtue, namely, avoidance of the extremes of too much or too little.

The virtue of temperance regulates and controls our sensate appetites and desires, in accordance with the axiom of St. Thomas Aquinas that the human passions and sensual desires are meant by nature to be obedient to reason. The difficulty is that the desire for the pleasure derived from food, drink or sex, for example, is such that once the pleasure is enjoyed, it is relatively easy to stimulate the desire to repeat the enjoyment. But sensual pleasure does not give complete and final satisfaction; it simply intensifies the desire for more. That is why it is so easy to acquire the vice of intemperance in food, drink or sexual pleasure.

These sensate desires arise from within; they are part of our human nature and are necessary for self-preservation (food and drink) and for the preservation of the species (procreation through sexual union). But the desire for selfish pleasure is so strong that one must exercise special vigilance and control over one's sensate desires, and especially over the sexual instinct. Thus, St. Paul told the Thessalonians to be faithful to the instructions he had given them: "It is God's will that you grow in holiness, that you abstain from immorality, each of you guarding his member in sanctity and honor, not in passionate desire as do the Gentiles who know not God" (2 Th 4:3-5).

Every Christian is obliged to maintain strict control over his sensual desires and pleasures. And St. Augustine has stated that of all the battles a Christian must wage in this spiritual warfare, the most severe attacks are the ones against the virtue of chastity. What makes it even more difficult is that it is not simply a question of preserving bodily chastity, but chastity of mind as well. Thus, Christ said: "You have heard the commandment, 'You shall not commit adultery.' What I say to you is: anyone who looks lustfully at a woman has already committed adultery with her in his thoughts" (Mt 5:27-28). In God's eyes it is all one, both the external deed and the intention to perform the act.

St. Jerome asks: "Who will glory in having a pure and chaste heart if he does not use all the safeguards to protect that purity?" The first and best safeguard of chastity is the practice of prayer, because a person who has the habit of prayer will most surely turn to God at the first stirring of the sexual urge. Another safeguard is the practice of abstinence and sobriety in the use of food and drink, for this makes it easier to control the movements of sensuality. Another great help is to observe custody of the external senses, for they are the gates through which enticing images come in contact with the soul, as happened when David gazed upon the beauty of Bathsheba (2 S 11:1-4). Finally, the general safeguard that applies to all the virtues is to avoid the occasions of sin, and in regard to the virtue of temperance, to stay away from those persons, places or things that may arouse the desire for sensual pleasure. Vigilance is absolutely necessary because, as St. Thomas Aquinas has stated, it is very easy to become habituated to the performance of acts that produce sensate satisfaction.

However, it is important to understand that although the temptation to sins against chastity may be very strong and cause great physical disturbance, it cannot prevail over you unless you give consent. We repeat the axiom of St. Thomas Aquinas: the lower powers and faculties are meant by nature to be obedient to reason. As long as you withhold consent, you have not sinned; as long as you resist, you have won the crown of victory. Consequently, at the first sign of danger, follow the example of the ancient monks for whom the most powerful prayer of petition was the invocation: "O God, come to my assistance; O Lord, make haste to help me!"

In regard to the pleasure of eating and drinking, we read in Scripture: "Remember that gluttony is evil.... Does not a little suffice for a well-bred man? In whatever you do, be moderate, and no sickness will befall you.... Let not wine-drinking be the proof of your strength, for wine has been the ruin of many.... Wine is very life to man if taken in moderation. Does he really live who lacks the wine which was created for his joy?" (Sir 31:13-27, passim).

If moderation is required in the matter of food, it is much more necessary in regard to drink, because wine and other intoxicating beverages can easily weaken the defenses to chastity. Hence St. Paul admonishes us: "Avoid getting drunk on wine; that leads to debauchery" (Eph 5:18). St. Jerome gives this warning to young people in particular: "Wine and youthfulness are two incentives to lust. Why throw oil on the fire? Why add more fuel to the flames?" Excessive drinking undoes the work of the moral virtues, whose primary purpose is to control the passions.

Nor should we neglect to mention that immoderate drinking and excessive eating can often lead to sins against justice. A person who has had too much to drink should refrain from talking too much or trusting others in his company. Many persons who have revealed too much while eating and drinking have later wished they had not spoken. Solomon says that there are no secrets in the kingdom of wine. It is said that St. Augustine was so opposed to the practice of talking about others that he had a short statement printed and placed in view of all at his table: "He who comes here to gnaw on the character of those who are absent, let him know that this table was not set for him."

The Christian who faithfully practices fasting and sobriety should realize that these are ways in which he can imitate Christ in a special way. As to those who are so sensate that they are not interested in anything but their own pleasure and gratification, we ask: What is more contrary to human dignity than excess in food and drink? A person who wishes to accomplish great things must be able to control his lower appetites and subject them to the rule of reason and the guidance of the virtues of temperance and prudence.

Some persons may say that the advice we have given on the virtue of temperance is suitable for monks and nuns but not for the average Christian. Those who live in the world should not be expected to practice the austerities that are observed in monasteries. My reply to them is to invite them to read the history of the Roman empire. When abstinence gave way to gluttony, sobriety to drunkenness, and chastity

to the pursuit of sexual pleasure, the ancient Romans became
soft and effeminate, corrupted by lust and satiated with food
and drink. What they had won by austerity and discipline, they
lost by their dissolute lives. The Romans had conquered the
civilized world, but in the end they were not able to control
their lust and inordinate appetites. This same disaster can befall any nation, society or individual when the virtue of temperance ceases to control the movements and demands of the
sensate appetite.

The Virtue of Fortitude

There are two obvious difficulties in the acquisition of
virtue: distinguishing between good and evil and overcoming
evil in order to attain the good. The one requires careful discernment and the other requires great fortitude. As long as
either of these conditions is lacking, virtue remains weak and
imperfect and the effort to attain it is significantly ineffectual.

The fortitude of which we are speaking is not simply the
particular virtue that suppresses fear and cowardice, but the
general virtue by which a person overcomes the difficulties
encountered in practicing any and all of the virtues required
for living the Christian life. Because of our innate weakness
and sloth, the faithful practice of virtue is difficult, but the virtue of fortitude can provide the patience and perseverance
needed to be faithful in the pursuit of perfection.

Whether it be a question of fasting, prayer, temperance,
obedience, humility or any other virtue, we always encounter
difficulties in faithfully following the path of virtue. The reasons for this are numerous: our innate self-centered love, the
temptations in our daily life, the allurements of the world, the
influence of the devil, and so forth. If fortitude is lacking, one
can accomplish little in the spiritual life, even if he has the

highest regard for the practice of the virtues. Such a person is as helpless as if he were bound hand and foot.

It is worth mentioning a great deception that often befalls those who are beginning to serve God faithfully. They read in spiritual books how sweet are the fruits of charity and how great are the consolations received from the Holy Spirit. They conclude from this that the path to perfection is filled with delights and there is no difficulty or effort involved. As a result, they enter upon the task in anticipation of the joy that comes from intimate union with God, but they fail to arm themselves for battle.

It is true that union with God is in itself sweet and delectable, but the road that leads to that degree of perfection is narrow and arduous. To reach it, one must conquer self-love completely, a task which calls for a radical conversion and purgation. But God bestows marvelous consolations on those who struggle valiantly to trade the delights of earthly pleasures for the joys of the spiritual life. If, however, a man does not want to make this barter because he is unwilling to give up his sinful attachments, he will not be able to "taste and see how good the Lord is" (Ps 34:9). That is why Scripture so often condemns sloth and indifference and praises fortitude so highly.

You may be wondering what means can be used in order to cultivate and perfect the virtue of fortitude. The first thing necessary is to be convinced of the importance of this virtue for the faithful practice of all the other virtues. Indeed, the very word "virtue" signifies power and strength. To help you see the importance of fortitude for living a virtuous life, just ask yourself why sensate worldly persons shy away from practicing the virtues of their state in life. Is it not because of the effort and self-denial that are necessary? The slothful man says: "Better is one handful with tranquility than two with toil" (Ec 11:8). But the kingdom of heaven is won only by the courageous, and the virtue of fortitude is very effective in overriding the selfish demands of self-centered love.

The practice of the virtue of fortitude is exemplified in the lives of the holy men and women who have persevered in the Christian life in spite of persecution and every kind of trial and temptation. Some of them embraced hardship and asceticism so ardently that they sought out the most rigorous and demanding lifestyle or the most challenging apostolate. And what is more opposed to the delights and pleasures of the world than the practice of the evangelical counsels of poverty, chastity and obedience? That kind of a life is completely contrary to life according to the flesh, but it is in complete accord with the spirit of the Lord.

More particularly, the example of the martyrs is a perpetual reminder of the need to detach ourselves from the pleasures and comforts of the flesh. Think of the suffering and torments they endured in order to gain the reward of eternal happiness in heaven. Scarcely a day passes that the Church does not propose for our remembrance the example of one or more martyrs whose names are listed in the Martyrology. Yet the martyrs had bodies that were not substantially different from our own. The same God was their helper, as he is ours; the same glory was offered to them as a reward, as it is to us. If they could endure so much for the love of God, how is it that we for the same love do not mortify our selfish desires?

If some of them died of starvation, can we not fast for one day? If they remained steadfast in the midst of their trials and sufferings, can we not spend an hour on our knees in prayer? If they willingly submitted to the instruments of torture and the attacks of wild beasts, shall we not control our passions and sensate desires? If they spent weeks, months or years in the darkness and cold of a prison cell, can we not spend some time with the Lord in the Blessed Sacrament or alone in our room? If they humbly submitted to scourging and beatings by their persecutors, shall we not carry the cross that God has placed on our shoulders?

And if the example of the martyrs is not enough to make you resolute in the practice of fortitude, then raise your eyes to the holy wood of the Cross and see who it is that suffers the agony of crucifixion. "Remember how he endured the opposition of sinners; hence, do not grow despondent or abandon the struggle. In your fight against sin you have not yet resisted to the point of shedding blood" (Heb 12:3-4).

The example of Christ crucified is a powerful one, no matter under which aspect we consider it. If we think of the effort and struggle involved, there was none greater; if we consider the Person who suffered, there was none more noble and holy; if we think of the reason why he suffered, it was not for any fault of his own, for he was innocent. He suffered out of goodness and love, and his suffering of body and soul was greater than the suffering endured by all the martyrs throughout the centuries. It was so great that it caused astonishment in heaven and made the earth quake.

How could some men be so unmoved by this when even inanimate creation reacted to the death of Christ on the cross? Christ said that it was fitting that he suffer these things because he came into the world for our redemption and salvation. But the way of Christ is the way of the Cross, and we are called to follow in his footsteps. His example gives us the courage to walk on the path that leads to Calvary and beyond to the kingdom of heaven.

Who would be such an ingrate and such a lover of his own ease and comfort that when he sees the Lord and his faithful disciples following the Way of the Cross, he would spend his life serving his own self-interest? Having seen the fidelity and generosity of the saints and of him who is the Saint of saints, I do not know by what right or title any Christian can lay claim to the privilege of reaching the same goal as they did by traveling along the path of pleasure and comfort.

Therefore, if you wish to be a companion of the saints in glory, you must also be their companion in self-denial and hardship. If you wish to reign with them, you must first serve an apprenticeship of suffering. Above all, remember the words of Christ: "Whoever wishes to be my follower must deny his very self, take up his cross each day, and follow in my steps" (Lk 9:23).

- 13 -

The Virtue of Religion

WHEN WE DISCUSSED the moral virtue of justice, we pointed out that it is a virtue that governs our relations with others. *Commutative justice* refers to relations with one's equals; *distributive justice* governs relations of superiors to inferiors; *legal justice* is concerned with the rights and duties of subjects towards their superiors. It is in this third type of justice that we find the virtue of religion, which governs our duties to almighty God. Note, however, that the virtue of religion is something distinct from the organized religion of a particular church or sect, the body of doctrine expressed in a creed, or the liturgical ceremonies in which church members worship God. Rather, we are here speaking of religion as a personal interior virtue that prompts the individual to worship almighty God.

By reason of its object — the worship of almighty God — the virtue of religion is the most excellent of all the moral virtues. And since God is the Creator of all things and we are his creatures, we have an obligation to give to God the honor and worship that is due to him. We read the "Great Commandment" in the Old Testament: "Hear, O Israel! The Lord is our God, the Lord alone! Therefore, you shall love the Lord, your God, with all your heart, and with all your soul, and with all your strength" (Dt 6:4-5).

According to St. Thomas Aquinas, there are numerous

particular acts listed under this virtue, but we shall speak only
of those that apply to the generality of Christians. And the first
of these acts or expressions of religion is called *devotion*. Many
persons think of it as a certain tenderness which prompts them
to turn to God in prayer or the sensible consolation that one
sometimes experiences in prayer or worship. But neither of
these things is devotion. As a matter of fact, a person in the
state of mortal sin could have feelings of consolation and tenderness towards God while a truly devout person may experience nothing but aridity and emptiness. Consequently, true
devotion is not a matter of feelings; it is a promptness of will
in fulfilling God's commandments and rendering to him the
obedience and worship that is his due. To put it in other words,
the devout Christian is one who is prompt and faithful in the
service of God.

It is true, of course, that feelings of devotion may accom-
pany prayer or the worship of God, but feelings as such are
not the measure of excellence or merit since, as we have said,
one may perform religious acts without the slightest feeling
of consolation, though they may be of great merit in God's
eyes. When Jesus prayed in the Garden of Gethsemane, his
heart was "nearly broken with sorrow" (Mt 26:38), but he rose
from his prayer with courageous determination to follow the
path willed for him by his heavenly Father.

It is true, however, that spiritual consolation makes the
Christian more prompt in serving God and in that way increases
true devotion. Understood in this way, devotion is a general
characteristic of the dedicated Christian; it disposes one for
the practice of prayer (love of God) and the performance of
the works of charity (love of neighbor).

We wish now to treat of the steps to perfect devotion.
This is equivalent to discussing the steps to perfect prayer and
contemplation or the highest degree of union with God that
is possible in this life. This spiritual doctrine was called *mystical theology* by some of the ancient theologians. It is not only

the most lofty branch of theology but it is also the most important, because the goal of our life is perfect union with God in glory.

The first thing required for the attainment of true devotion and perseverance in prayer is a *sincere and efficacious desire*. The reason for this is that it is the desire to attain an end or goal that sets the whole process in motion; and the more intense the desire, the greater the care and diligence with which one strives to reach the goal. See how avaricious or ambitious persons conduct themselves. They can think of nothing else by day or night except how they can succeed in their self-centered efforts. If this is true in regard to purely natural and secular pursuits, it is all the more so in regard to growth in virtue and the love of God. It is written that the kingdom of God suffers violence and the violent take it by force (Mt 11:12).

Consequently, desire must be accompanied by *great diligence and fortitude* so that we can overcome the obstacles and difficulties that threaten the success of our striving. Many persons have good and holy desires but lack the courage to put them into effect. Such persons are either slothful or they are wishful thinkers, as Scripture says: "The soul of the sluggard craves in vain, but the diligent soul is amply satisfied" (Pr 13:4). When they consider the beauty of virtue, they crave it, but when they see the difficulty and effort involved in putting it into practice, they no longer desire it.

We should also note that while our desires must be carried into action with fortitude lest they be inefficacious, our fortitude must be accompanied by *humility* lest we become proud and self-sufficient. We should exert our best efforts and do the best we can, but we should do so with the understanding that it is not so much our personal efforts but God's grace and mercy that enable us to make progress in the spiritual life. So we read in Ecclesiastes: "The race is not won by the swift, nor the battle by the valiant, nor a livelihood by the wise, nor riches by the shrewd, nor favor by the experts" (Ec 9:11). Grace is given to the humble, and in this respect humility is more important than courage in attaining our goal.

Another important aid for cultivating the practice of prayer and true devotion is to observe *custody of the senses and passions*. The external senses are the gateways through which sensate images enter our interior and stimulate the passions. We cannot avoid these contacts in our daily life but we can stand guard at the gateways and turn away those sense impressions that will distract us unduly or tempt us to some thought, word or deed that is unworthy of a Christian. Those who keep a watch over their senses and passions will be able more readily to achieve the recollection that is proper to a devout, prayerful Christian.

Those, on the other hand, who spend their time in worldly pastimes and are interested only in mundane matters will have minds filled with air, lacking devotion. They are vagabonds at heart and restless in body and soul. They cannot sit still for a moment or remain at a task for any length of time. They must be constantly running here and there, from one place to another, and when they have no place in particular to go, they will follow their whim or fancy to find some distraction or amusement. They have lost the ability to find peace and contentment in solitude, recollection and prayer.

St. Bernard says: "You will have solitude if you do not harbor common and vulgar thoughts, if you do not desire present goods, if you disdain the things that the world holds dear. You will be able to reject what the world desires if you keep yourself from contention, if you take no account of temporal losses and gains, and if you do not reckon with injuries. Otherwise, although you may be alone, you will not enjoy true solitude."

There are many paths and ways by which a Christian may travel to perfection and there are many subjects for prayer and meditation by which he can raise his mind and heart to God.

Each individual should determine what is most helpful and best suited to himself, after taking into account the circumstances and his own disposition and personal need. Once having decided, one must be faithful in carrying out the decision to completion. At the same time, one should realize that it is an error to conclude that because a method has worked for one individual it should be applied to all. The truth is that there are many pathways that lead to God. The Holy Spirit is the primary director of souls and he will lead each person by the way that is best suited and most beneficial.

The first thing necessary is to rid the mind of all vain and useless thoughts. The mind and heart of the sensate man is like a busy thoroughfare or the public square; it is always occupied and busy, day and night; but the devout soul is like an enclosed garden. Next, one must keep the passions and affections under control. They fill the mind with distractions, arouse inordinate affections, and lead to slavish attachments.

Those who live under the sway of their emotions are as fickle and changeable as a weather vane. Such persons will never possess a stable and balanced character. Now they are happy, now they are sad; now peaceful, now disturbed; now serious, now giddy; now devout, now dissolute. They are like the chameleon, which changes its color to suit its environment. Scripture advises us: "Ever wise are the discourses of the devout, but the godless man, like the moon, is inconstant. Limit the time you spend among fools, but frequent the company of thoughtful men" (Si 27:11-12).

In order to preserve custody of the heart and the emotions, one should strive always to live in the presence of God, not only during prayer time but in every time and place. Some Christians are like children at school; during class time they are attentive and well-behaved, but as soon as the class ends, they scatter in whatever direction their whims may take them. Devout souls, on the other hand, will rise from their prayer and go about their duties in a spirit of recollection. And in

order to maintain this prayerful and recollected spirit, it helps
to realize that God is present in every place and moment,
because he not only created all things but he preserves them
in existence. So St. Paul says: "For from him and through him
and for him all things are" (Rm 11:36).

Speak to the Lord frequently throughout the day, even
when you are engaged in the work of your hands or with other
occupations that do not require your undivided attention. Little
by little you will cultivate the habit of recollection. At the beginning it is helpful to make use of the short prayers and in-
vocations that were used by the monks and hermits as they
performed their manual labor. Examples of this type of ejaculatory prayer are the petition "My Jesus mercy"; the invocation "O Lord, make haste to help me"; the "Glory be to the
Father"; or the simple repetition of the name of Jesus or Mary.
Yet another great help is to cultivate the habit of regular spiritual reading, and especially the attentive reading of Scripture.
St. Jerome once wrote in a letter to the consecrated virgin
Demetria: "Love Scripture, and wisdom will love you; give
yourself to it and it will protect you; embrace it and it will
honor you."

To conclude our consideration of the aids to true devotion and the practice of prayer, we should say a word about
the time, place and manner best suited for devotion and prayer.
St. Bernard said that a quiet and peaceful time is best suited
for prayer, because then one can be more attentive. And Scripture says that "one must give you thanks before the sunrise,
and turn to you at daybreak" (Ws 16;28). Consequently, early
morning and late evening would seem to be the most suitable time for prayer. Of course, one may have to use a different time if old age, sickness or one's duties dictate otherwise.
Ultimately the best time for prayer is the time in which an
individual can best pray. Moreover, a solitary and quiet place
is most conducive to prayer. We read in Scripture that Jesus
was accustomed to go off by himself to a secluded place in

order to pray and in so doing he was giving us an example to follow. Finally, the light should be subdued, because St. Antony of the desert stated that the brilliance of the rising sun impeded his contemplation of God.

Yet another question has to do with bodily posture. First and foremost, one should normally follow the customs of his or her liturgical rite or national custom. For example, in the Western Church the faithful usually kneel for public prayer and private devotions; in the Eastern Church the usual posture is to stand. But for mental prayer such as meditation, prudence dictates that a person assume a posture in which it is easiest to meditate, whether sitting, kneeling or walking. Few people can pray for any length of time in an uncomfortable position; the practice of prayer then becomes a penitential exercise. As regards the length of time spent in prayer, St. Thomas Aquinas gave a succinct, practical directive: *as long as devotion lasts.* Accordingly, the period of prayer will depend entirely on the individual, unless it is a question of public community prayer or prayers that are of obligation.

Since union with God is the goal of our Christian life, we should exert great effort to achieve this by cooperating with the graces that God gives us. This is the "better part" that was chosen by Mary of Bethany; it is the work of the contemplative life, which is much more excellent than the active life (Lk 10:41). St. Thomas Aquinas has said that the interior act of charity is the most excellent and most meritorious of all the acts of all the virtues. The practice of the love of God will teach you more in one hour than all the masters can teach you in a lifetime. Scripture tells us: "Though one be perfect among the sons of men, if Wisdom, who comes from you, be not with him, he shall be held in no esteem" (Ws 9:6).

- 14 -

Vocal Prayer

PRAYER, AS THE SPIRITUAL WRITERS tell us, is the raising of our minds and hearts to God. It lifts the soul above created things to unite it to God; it enables the soul to go forth to God, whom it approaches with God's grace; it helps prepare the soul to become a temple of God's indwelling in order to love and possess him. Prayer places a soul in the presence of God; it is a spiritual dialogue in which the soul, seated at the feet of God, listens to his teaching and responds to his grace.

St. Bonaventure tells us that during prayer God inflames the soul with his love and anoints it with his grace. And once anointed, it is spiritually elevated; and being lifted up, it contemplates him; and contemplating him, it loves him; loving him, it tastes and sees that the Lord is sweet; and it reposes in him. In this sweet repose is found the greatest glory that can be attained in this life.

Prayer is a salutary healing of each day's imperfections, a daily exercise of the virtues, a silencing of the demands of the sensate appetite and the origin of all good desires and intentions. It is milk for the beginners, solid food for the advanced, and the reward of those who have triumphed in the spiritual warfare. Prayer is medicine for the sick, strength for the weak, a remedy for sin, fraternal support for the living, suffrage for the dead, and a blessing for the entire Church.

Anyone who sincerely wants to travel along the road to perfection, root out vices and cultivate the virtues, will find that the practice of prayer opens the door to everything else. And one of the greatest blessings that derive from the faithful practice of prayer is that it stimulates the activity of the virtues of the Christian life. St. Bonaventure writes very beautifully on prayer in the following statements:

> If you want to bear the trials and adversities of life with patience, be a man of prayer. If you want to acquire virtue and the strength to overcome temptations, be a man of prayer. If you wish to mortify the inclinations and desires of your will, be a man of prayer. If you wish to know the wiles of Satan in order to defend yourself against him, be a man of prayer. If you wish to live joyfully and travel with ease along the path of penance and good works, be a man of prayer. If you wish to rid your soul of the pestilence of vain thoughts and anxieties, be a man of prayer. If you wish the support of solid devotion to keep your soul filled with good thoughts and desires, be a man of prayer. If you want to strengthen your heart on the road to God, be a man of prayer. If you want to rid your soul of all its vices and plant in it the flowers of the virtues, be a man of prayer.

We read in Scripture: "All you who are thirsty, come to the water!" (Is 55:1). Come, all of you, from every state and condition of life, to drink from this fountain! If you are a sinner, you will learn how to repent of your sins. If you are a just Christian, you will be more justified still. If you are beset with doubts and anxieties, you will find peace; if you are lukewarm and indifferent, you will be inspired by God's grace. If you are sad and afflicted, your soul will find rest.

Are you a priest or religious? Then most likely the practice of prayer was one of the factors that attracted you to that vocation. If you are a married person, the practice of prayer is a help in bearing the burdens of your state in life. Are you a child? Then in prayer you will find security in the protective arms of your heavenly Father. Are you an adult? Then in the practice of prayer you will find the courage to profess your faith by practicing the Christian virtues. And whether you wish to acquire wisdom or be more humble and charitable, you will achieve it through the practice of prayer. There are no greater gifts under the heavens than those which can be received through prayer.

There are two types of prayer: prayer of the lips, which is *vocal prayer*, and prayer of the heart and mind, or *mental prayer*, which we use when we attentively consider the things of God and present our needs to the Lord, to whom the language of the heart is as intelligible as language of the tongue.

Vocal prayer is beneficial for all classes of people, but especially for beginners, if it is recited with the proper attention and devotion. Consequently, those who because of lack of knowledge do not have material on which to meditate or those who through lack of devotion do not have words of their own with which to pray, can make use of the words of others to raise their minds and hearts to God. Vocal prayer is useful not only for beginners, however; it also helps the advanced souls and the more perfect, especially when the distraction of their duties or the indisposition of illness make it impossible for them to practice their customary mental prayer. At such times they can stimulate their devotion by using the short vocalized prayers of which we have spoken or by using a prayer-book. It is said that some days before his death, St. Augustine had the seven penitential psalms written out and hung on the wall near his bed so that he could read them, which he did, shedding copious tears. In like manner, those who live the monastic life have traditionally chanted the psalms of the breviary so that the sweetness of the melody of the chant would penetrate the heart and awaken devotion. Music is naturally delightful and pleasing to the soul. Even the restless infant in the mother's arms is pacified and put to rest by her soft singing of a lullaby.

But although the beautiful words and sentiments of vocal prayer are helpful in awakening true devotion, they may become an impediment once devotion is aroused. The reason for this is that once the soul has been moved to acts of love for God or admiration and thanksgiving for his many blessings, the soul may want to remain for a time in that state and not move on to the next section of vocalized prayer. When a person begins to experience the delight and consolation of true devotion, the tongue becomes silent and the powers and faculties of the soul tend to focus on the experience of God's presence. It is an experience that is too deep for words.

When the soul finds itself in this condition and realizes that the reading or recitation of vocal prayer is more of a hindrance than a help, it should put aside the vocal prayer. The words of the vocal prayer were instrumental in arousing devotion, but it would be unreasonable to let the means become an obstacle to the very purpose for which it was used. Therefore, when a person comes upon a passage in spiritual reading or in a prayer-book that stirs one's devotion and promises spiritual consolation, it is a mistake to pass on and continue reading.

That would be to run away from the very thing that one seeks in prayer, for one of the reasons for praying is to foster true devotion, and vocal prayer is of more or less benefit to the extent that it serves to accomplish that end. Of course, this advice applies only to one's *personal private prayer,* in the case of public liturgical prayer or community prayer it is not possible to stop the recitation of the prayer in order to savor the sweetness of one's personal devotion.

It is an axiom in philosophy that a cause produces its effect in proportion to the disposition of the subject on which it acts. Thus, fire will burn more brightly and with greater intensity if the wood is dry; an impression made on wax will be more clearly defined if the wax is soft but sufficiently firm. Now God is the first and universal cause of all things and the dispenser of all grace. In accordance with the principle just given, a person will receive grace in proportion to his disposition and receptivity. And one of the most powerful means for disposing oneself for the reception of grace is the practice of prayer.

Moreover, it is in the practice of prayer that the devout Christian can experience the joy and security of union with God. It is a union that is attained not by steps of the body but of the spirit, and the more intimate the union, the greater is the sharing in the nature and life of God. Thus, St. Augustine says that we approach God, not by walking, but by loving; not with steps of the body, but by movements of the heart.

If we consider the matter further, we discover that the practice of prayer sustains the spiritual life. The reason for this is that the spiritual life consists essentially and primarily in the love that is charity. And what is of greater help in preserving charity than frequent consideration of the divine perfections and conversation with him who loves us?

Not only does the practice of prayer sustain the spiritual life; it also enables the devout Christian to taste and see that the Lord is good. This is the work of the Holy Spirit, the Paraclete and Consoler, who fills the soul with such wondrous spiritual delights that it readily disdains all mundane pleasures. God uses this procedure to wean the soul from the things of earth. St. Bernard has said that once the soul experiences spiritual delights, all other pleasures become insipid and tasteless.

We have seen that the practice of prayer disposes the soul for the reception of grace, leads to a more intimate union with God in charity, and raises the mind to the contemplation of the divine beauty. It nourishes the virtues, sheds light on the truths of the faith, and delights the soul with the spiritual consolations that flow from contemplative prayer. If a Christian conscientiously and faithfully practices prayer, his entire life will become integrated and properly ordered, his conscience will be purified, and his soul will be filled with good intentions and holy resolutions. Gradually he will become more and more aware of living in the presence of God and of experiencing the power of grace working through him. It is as if he is now being carried on the wings of eagles, for the Holy Spirit is now leading his soul along the pathway to sanctity at an increasing rate of speed.

It is often remarkable to see the dramatic change that occurs when a person begins to practice prayer seriously and faithfully. A person may be distraught, vivacious, depressed or indifferent, but even after a relatively short time in the daily practice of prayer, the change may be so great that he seems like a different person. If a plant is not watered, it will soon begin to wither and eventually die, but pour some water on it and you will see that almost immediately the stem will become erect and the leaves will regain their shape and color. This is what the practice of prayer can do for the soul that is drying up for lack of the spiritual irrigation of grace.

Many nuns and monks are enclosed in the security of their cloistered life and are faithful in the observances of their religious life. Each day they are at the table of the Lord to be nourished by his Body and Blood in the Eucharist; they are conscientious in attending the daily choral recitation of the Divine Office; they observe the practices prescribed by their Constitutions. Nevertheless, if these same religious are negligent in the practice of daily mental prayer, they can become so dry, so remiss and lukewarm that little by little they will turn back to the interests and preoccupations of a completely secular life. They will have lost their taste for the lifestyle of a religious. The same thing can happen to a diocesan priest, and for the same reason, namely, neglect of his personal mental prayer.

On the other hand, you may meet a wife and mother who is burdened with the care and nurturing of children and the daily performance of numerous household duties. She doesn't have the free time to engage in the pious exercises of a monk or nun; the duties of her state in life do not permit it. Nevertheless, she does manage to find time each day for her private prayer and to assist at Mass occasionally during the week.

She may possess such a high degree of charity and patience, such dedication to her duties as a wife and mother, such a disregard for worldly or selfish satisfaction, that we are embarrassed and ashamed that we do not measure up as well to our own obligations. How is it that so many priests and religious can be so dry and lukewarm in the midst of their religious observances while a woman burdened with many cares can become so holy without using any of those same exercises?

One could think of many reasons, but I am convinced that a principal reason is her spirit of true devotion and her faithful practice of prayer. It goes without saying that if the practice of prayer is so important for sustaining one's spiritual life and growing in grace, the abandonment of daily personal prayer will most certainly lead to lukewarmness and ultimately the neglect of one's duties of state in life. If anyone does not believe this, let him test this doctrine by spending a period of time in personal mental prayer each day. He will soon discover that what we have said about the necessity and value of daily personal prayer is no exaggeration.

We can see from this the error of those religious who concentrate exclusively on activity and external observances without balancing the active life with the interior life of prayer. Such religious should realize that the observances of religious life, public liturgical prayer and the works of the apostolate are meant to draw souls to greater perfection and union with God. This is the sense in which the contemplative life should be the crown of the active life. Otherwise, what does it profit a person to expend all one's energy in external practices and neglect the growth of the interior life? Jesus condemned the

Pharisees for that very thing. They scrupulously observed the dead letter of the law and ignored the spirit. And that is legalism in the worst sense of the word.

Some persons may tell you that if you conscientiously perform the external works of your state in life, that will suffice also for your practice of prayer, because then your work is your prayer. This is not what Christ meant when he told us to pray always. He not only explicitly commanded us to pray, but he gave us an example of personal private prayer. If he had meant that good works or love of neighbor could replace the practice of prayer, he would have said so. The conclusion we draw is that one will seldom work well who does not pray well.

Obviously, we cannot pray always in a literal sense; that would be psychologically impossible because of the limitations of our human nature. We should use common sense in interpreting such a statement. Christ is not asking us to attempt the impossible, but to pray as frequently as we can, in view of our state in life and our other duties and commitments. It follows from this that there can be no universal rule that applies to all. Some persons can and need to spend more time in prayer; others less so. In the initial grades of prayer one needs to go to God more frequently with prayers of petition to the heavenly Father; but when one's prayer has become the language of love, the devout soul is once again drawn to God as to a beloved friend.

Let us now consider the requisites for prayer, and the first one is that we should pray with *attention*. Jesus said that when we pray we should withdraw into our chamber and pray in secret to our heavenly Father. In other words, he wants us to rid our souls of all worldly cares and thoughts so that we can fix our minds and hearts on God in silent recollection. For prayer is conversation with God and we should therefore pay close attention to what we are saying or thinking and the God whom we are addressing. Cassian has said: "He prays little who prays only when he is on his knees, and he prays not at all who, although he is on his knees, is voluntarily distracted." St. John Chrysostom said something similar: "If you do not hear your own prayer, how can you expect God to hear it? You say that you are on your knees in church. That may be true, but your mind is wandering all over the world. Your mouth may be speaking to God, but you could even be thinking evil thoughts."

However, if distractions are not voluntary but arise of their own accord, one should pray as best he can in spite of the distracting thoughts. Our human weakness is such that we cannot keep all our thoughts and feelings under our control at all times. Remember that the practice of prayer has three distinct benefits: merit, impetration and devotion. Only the third requires actual attention; for merit and impetration, good will and the proper intention suffice. This should be a great consolation to those persons who do their best to pray in the midst of distractions. In the sight of God, their action is still meritorious and their petitions do rise to God.

The second requisite for the practice of prayer is *true humility*. Scripture tells us: "The prayer of the lowly pierces the clouds; it does not rest until it reaches its goal, nor will it withdraw till the Most High responds, judges justly and affirms the right" (Si 35:17-18). Humility enables a person to recognize his own weakness and need so that he can call out to God: "O God, come to my assistance. O Lord, make haste to help me." This is the spirit in which Christ himself prayed when he prostrated himself on the ground in the Garden of Gethsemane. If he who is without sin humbled himself before his heavenly Father, he did so in order to teach us how to pray.

The third requisite for prayer is *faith and confidence*. If the virtue of humility teaches us not to rely on ourselves alone, the virtue of faith teaches us to trust in God. In fact, the very word faith (*fides*) connotes confidence or trust. Hence, St.

James advises us to "petition the Lord with faith, never doubting, because the doubter cannot expect to receive anything from the Lord" (Jm 1:6). And Jesus has told us: "You will receive all that you ask for, provided you have faith" (Mt 21:22).

But now you may ask how you can have that kind of faith and confidence when you have done so little for God. The answer is that the basis for faith and confidence is not what you have done for God, but the goodness and mercy of God and the merits of the passion and death of Jesus Christ. Remember, God is infinite and so also is his mercy. Therefore, when you approach God with your petitions, do not be timid or afraid. He is our Father and we are his children; in asking him with childlike confidence to grant us what we need, we are giving glory to God. Moreover, when we ask in Jesus' name, we are professing our faith that Jesus Christ is our Redeemer and Mediator.

But faith alone is not sufficient, as St. James tells us. "What good is it to profess faith without practicing it? Such faith has no power to save one, has it? ... You must perceive that a person is justified by his works and not by faith alone" (Jm 2:14, 24). In his infinite mercy, God sometimes hears the prayer of a sinner and grants his petition, but normally, as the man cured of blindness said: "We know that God does not hear sinners, but that if someone is devout and obeys his will, he listens to him" (Jn 9:31). In other words, our prayers and petitions should be *reinforced by penitential acts and the practice of the virtues proper to our state of life.* We learn from the example of the saints of the Old Testament and the traditional teaching of Christian spiritual masters that *fasting and almsgiving* hold a high place among the works of self-denial.

Yet another consideration in the prayer of petition pertains to the subject matter of our requests: for what should we pray? First and foremost we should ask God for whatever pertains to our eternal salvation and growth in holiness. This is God's will for us, that we be holy and blameless in his sight and attain to union with him in glory. The temporal goods of this world may also be the object of our prayers, insofar as they contribute to our spiritual life and salvation. But ultimately we should always try to leave these things in God's hands. He knows best what is best for us, and for that reason our sentiment should be: "Thy will be done."

The last requisite for true prayer is *patience and perseverance.* Jesus gave us an example of this in the parable about the man who knocked at the door of his friend's house in the middle of the night. Although the friend tried to excuse himself by saying that he and his family were already in bed, the persistence of the man at the door made him get up and grant his request. The moral of the parable is that we should persevere in our prayer until we get an answer. This does not mean, however, that by perseverance we shall always obtain what we request. We know from experience that sometimes the answer to prayer is negative. For that reason St. Augustine taught that in all our petitions we should pray that God's will be done.

- 15 -

Mental Prayer

UP TO THIS POINT WE HAVE been discussing vocal prayer, and especially the prayer of petition, which is the type of prayer most generally used by the faithful and by the Church in the liturgy and the administration of the sacraments. Now we turn our attention to mental prayer, which is normally the type of personal prayer practiced by more advanced souls. Beginners in the practice of prayer need vocal prayers in order to converse with God, whether they be formulas of prayer that have been memorized or the prayers they read in a prayer-book or missal. But once they have made some progress in the spiritual life and have acquired some devotion, their love of God prompts them to find ways of expressing their sentiments in a more personal and intimate way.

Whether vocal or mental, all prayer is excellent and meritorious as an act of the virtue of religion. As one's devotion increases, the type of prayer practiced habitually by the individual will likewise rise from vocalized prayer to mental prayer and eventually to contemplation. But the best form of prayer for an individual here and now is that which is accompanied by the greatest devotion, whether one is praying from a book, with beads, or reciting a prayer from memory. Objectively, there are grades of prayer that are more or less excellent, but subjectively the best form of prayer is that in which the individual can best pray.

Mental prayer can be described as any form of meditation or consideration of one or another aspect of the spiritual life, even when one does not actually petition God for anything. There are various types of mental prayer; for example, the *ascetical grades*: discursive meditation, affective prayer, prayer of simple regard (acquired contemplation); and the *mystical grades*: infused contemplation, prayer of quiet and the degrees of prayer of union. Discursive meditation is the first and lowest grade of mental prayer and it is a most effective way of stimulating true devotion and the practice of the Christian virtues. In this type of mental prayer we look at ourselves by means of an examination of conscience in order to acquire true self-knowledge. We cannot make progress in the spiritual life unless we know how we stand before God and then take the practical steps to grow in the practice of virtue.

Another great benefit of discursive meditation is that it gives us a deeper awareness of divine things. In the recitation or reading of vocal prayer, we pass quickly and lightly over the words, but in meditation we can pause and mull over the words or concepts without being concerned about when we shall finish or whether we shall cover a specified amount of matter. In ancient monasticism the monks could spend the time in a leisurely consideration of a word or sentence. Similarly, if the Rosary is said properly, the attention is fixed on one of the mysteries in the life of Jesus and Mary while the words simply serve as a kind of mantra. In spiritual reading one can pass easily from the words on the page to a prayerful meditation on what one has been reading. We are told that St. Francis of Assisi could spend a whole night repeating the prayer: "Lord, that I may know you and that I may know myself."

It is perfectly permissible for a person to make discursive meditation with the help of a book, as long as it is done correctly. One should read along until coming upon a passage that is inspiring; then pause and think about it for as long as it is profitable. Even without using a book, some persons are able to move slowly through the recitation of the Our Father, pausing frequently to absorb more deeply the meaning of the words. In this way they resemble the humming birds that go from flower to flower to sip the nectar, or like persons sauntering through an art gallery and pausing every now and then before a striking painting. This type of meditation is eminently practical; it increases our understanding of spiritual truths and it prompts us to apply them to our lives and make firm resolutions for the future.

Since mental prayer deals with spiritual truths, it may be helpful to enumerate some particular points that are helpful for making a good meditation. Any subject is suitable as long as it arouses in us a love or holy fear of God, hatred for sin, disdain for the pleasures of this world, or any similar sentiments. Therefore, Sacred Scripture, the lives of the saints, or the spiritual writings of the great masters are excellent reading material. St. Thomas Aquinas mentions two topics in particular that are especially suitable for arousing devotion: the perfections of God and our own sinfulness and misery. The first, since it dwells on the perfection and goodness of God, prompts us to love him; the second, since it treats of our own weakness and guilt, fosters the virtues of humility, repentance and trust in God's mercy.

There are five steps to be followed in the practice of discursive meditation: preparation, spiritual reading, the meditation itself, thanksgiving, and petition. First of all, is *preparation*. Just as it is necessary to tune a stringed instrument before playing it, so also one should dispose oneself properly for mental prayer. Look first to the proper time and place. Usually the early morning hours are the best time, before one gets involved in the activities and duties of the day, and the best place is the one in which there will be the least noise and distraction. Then, having made the sign of the cross, we should focus our attention on what we are about to do, which is to come into the divine presence in order to converse with God. To this end, it would be well to recite an act of contrition or a psalm such as the *De profundis* in order to place ourselves in the proper frame of mind. However, one should not delay too long at this point; this is not the time to make an examination of conscience, but simply to renew one's sorrow for sin.

Having prepared oneself, the next step is to take up the book of spiritual reading in order to select the material for meditation. This is especially important for beginners, who have not yet become accustomed to recollection and spiritual considerations. Later on they will find that a book is no longer necessary.

The actual reading should not be done hurriedly but slowly and with great attention. When a particular statement or passage makes an impression, one should close the book and think about what has been read. Yet, one should not spend so much of the prayer time with spiritual reading that there is no time left for mental prayer. Of course, if a person is unable to concentrate sufficiently in order to meditate, then spiritual reading will at least keep the mind attentive to the things of God. If one cannot have white bread, then any kind of bread will have to do.

As a person becomes more proficient in the practice of mental prayer, spiritual reading or the study of sacred doctrine will be more and more separated from the practice of prayer, if only because the more advanced grades of mental prayer approach more and more closely to contemplation, which is a gaze of love rather than an intellectual pursuit.

After the spiritual reading comes the meditation proper. We should note here that sometimes the material of the meditation can be represented by the imagination, as when we dwell on a scene or event from the life of Christ, Mary or a particular saint. This is what happens when a person makes the Stations of the Cross or meditates on the mysteries of the

Rosary. At other times, one may make greater use of the intellect, as when we meditate on an attribute of God or the description of a particular virtue. What is especially important is to meditate on the subject matter in such a way that we make it vivid and meaningful to us. To put it another way, there are three questions one should ask and answer during the meditation proper: What does it mean? What does it mean to me? What am I going to do about it? Consequently, the three essential acts in any meditation are consideration, application, resolution.

Once the three acts of meditation are completed, we should give thanks to God for the benefits received. St. Paul exhorts us: "Pray perseveringly, be attentive to prayer, and pray in a spirit of thanksgiving" (Col 4:2). And St. Augustine says: "What greater thing could we think in the mind, speak with the mouth, or write with the pen, than 'Thanks be to God'? Nothing is more quickly said, more pleasing to the ear, more joyfully understood or more beneficially done."

The final act, that of petition, brings us back to the practice of vocal prayer, which we use throughout our whole life. It is closely connected with thanksgiving because we should not only thank God for benefits and graces received personally, but we should immediately pray that we may receive the grace to persevere in the spiritual life. At this point we should also petition God concerning our own particular needs, whether temporal or spiritual. Then we should expand our petition to pray for all the members of the Church, both the devout and sinners, both the living and the dead. Moreover, we should pray for the intentions of the Holy Father and the conversion of the world.

We shall now conclude our discussion with some general observations concerning mental prayer. In general, we can answer the questions concerning the appropriate subject matter, the best time, the best place, the most suitable posture, etc., by saying that we should decide these particulars in ac-

cordance with our own personal spiritual needs and the circumstances that will enable us to pray more devoutly. Two
extremes are to be avoided: the slavish and inflexible adher-
ence to a particular style or method, and the fickle and inconstant changing from one method to another. As long as we
are deriving spiritual profit, we should hold to the methods
we are using.

Second, we should *avoid too much speculation* in our
mental prayer. It is true, of course, that the functioning of the
intellect is required in order that the will may be guided and
instructed as to its choices. The goal of mental prayer, however, is to arouse true devotion, which is a virtue that operates in the will and produces the affections and spiritual sentiments that are the fruits of love of God. But too much intellectual activity changes the period of prayer into a study period, with the result that the activity of the will and the affections is minimal. Consequently, to meditate on the divine truths
in order to learn theology or prepare a sermon is a praise-
worthy activity, and it has its place, but it is not mental prayer.
The intellect must ponder the truths that are the subject matter of the meditation and then offer them to the will and the
affections so that they can be tasted and can stimulate devotion and holy desires. This being so, devout but uneducated
persons sometimes gain much more profit from their mental
prayer because they do not spend their time in pure speculation. Their primary exercise in mental prayer is loving. If you
want to learn how to do this, whenever you experience some
holy thought or ardent desire during prayer, immediately go
with it to God, as a loving child runs to its mother as soon as
it finds something.

On the other hand, we should not let the will and the
affections become too active or too ardent. The devotion we
seek is not obtained by force and exertion, as some seem to
think who work themselves into an emotional state in their
meditation. Such antics do nothing but impede true devotion

and foster a morbid desire for sensate religious experience. If the Lord grants the gift of tears, spiritual elevations or any other consolation in prayer, one should accept it with all humility, but it is imprudent and even dangerous to try to seize such things by force. One should be content with doing one's best to cooperate with the grace God gives and not reach for something the Lord has not granted.

In conclusion, it is well to avoid intense sensible feelings connected with the practice of prayer, and if they should arise spontaneously, one should try to keep them at arm's length. Devotion will last for a long time and its consolation will be more profound if the sensible feelings are moderated and controlled. Antics such as groans and sighs usually do nothing but dim the interior light and impede the work of the Holy Spirit. Beginners must be especially careful not to be overwhelmed by the novelty of sensible consolations in prayer. After they have made some progress in mental prayer and are accustomed to the practice of recollection, their love will have become more intense but it will no longer experience such sensible fervor and ecstatic delight.

Another point to be noted is the proper attention during mental prayer. There is no doubt that prayer in general requires that one be attentive to the exercise of prayer and to God, to whom all prayer should be addressed. Two extremes should be avoided: excessive effort in concentrating and laxity or slothfulness. Attention in prayer should not be so forced that we end up concentrating on self rather than on God, and it should not be so slight that we let our mind and imagination wander wherever they will. Some persons have practiced mental prayer for years, but with little profit, because they never exercised the attentiveness that is required for authentic prayer. They may have been physically present at prayer, but they were not praying.

Another important counsel is that one should never lose heart or abandon the practice of prayer if one does not experience the devotion that is desired. Sometimes the human heart is like muddied water, which cannot be cleared up suddenly, no matter how hard one tries. In fact, the effort only makes matters worse. It takes time for the sediment to settle before the water can become clear again.

So also, our hearts become muddied by the duties and distractions of daily life; we have to take the time to become properly disposed for the practice of mental prayer. "If it delays, wait for it, it will surely come, it will not be late" (Hab 2:3). But if the individual feels that it is time wasted because nothing is happening, then it would be advisable to turn to spiritual reading in order to stimulate one's devotion. This is a very profitable solution and it is especially useful for beginners.

It is also important not to become impatient, for it usually takes some time to settle down for a period of mental prayer. When the prayer period is preceded by some religious exercise such as the Divine Office, the Mass or some devotional ceremony, the mind is usually already calmed down, and the same thing is true if the mental prayer is practiced early in the morning, before the day's activities begin. As a rule it is more beneficial to have one long period of mental prayer rather than two short periods. The reason is that if only a brief time is allotted for mental prayer, it may happen that by the time a person gets into the mood for it, it is time to get up and go. Of course, there are many persons who are so occupied with their daily duties that they just do not have the leisure for lengthy periods of mental prayer or spiritual reading. Those persons should simply do the best they can, which is to make use of short, ejaculatory prayers throughout the day and trying their best to be aware of the presence of God. And if at such a time God should make his presence felt, one should immediately be attentive to the Lord, because more progress can be made in such a moment than in several days.

If we do not open when the Lord knocks, then perhaps he will not open to us the next time we knock. We repeat the admonition not to abandon the practice of prayer because of the lack of consolation. No matter how dry and fruitless it seems, one should try to wait upon the Lord. And if the prayer lacks consolations, it is well to remember that the things that are good for us are not necessarily pleasant and enjoyable. In fact, there is nothing remarkable in the fact that a person remains faithful and attentive to mental prayer when it is accompanied by consolations. But if one does the best he can to dispose himself for prayer, in spite of aridity, then he has done his part and can rest assured that God will reward his good intention.

- 16 -

Spiritual Consolations

Since the goal is the determining factor in human actions and objective morality, if a person makes a mistake in this regard, he will also be mistaken in regard to everything else. For that reason it is important to recognize that the goal of the Christian life is to attain to perfect union with God through obedience to his precepts under the impetus of charity. Jesus himself linked these two virtues together: "If you love me and obey the commands I give you, I will ask the Father and he will give you another Paraclete" (Jn 14:15-16). Consequently, perfect obedience and perfect charity are interchangeable terms because he who truly loves cannot help but obey what the beloved asks, and he will not obey unless he loves.

Obedience requires some degree of mortification and submission of our own will, because we cannot give the divine will first place in our hearts unless we deny our own will, and this calls for mortification and the practice of the moral virtues. That is why the practice of prayer is so important in our spiritual life, not only for what it is in itself — an act of the virtue of religion, which is the most excellent of all the moral virtues — but because of the help it gives us in achieving union with God. Under this aspect, prayer is not an end in itself but a means to the end or goal, just as medicine is a means for regaining one's health. Thus, a person may be much given to the practice of prayer but in spite of this, he may not be more virtuous or mortified. Such a person is like a sick man who is always taking medicine but never gets better.

We have already emphasized the necessity of not seeking delights and consolations in the practice of prayer. Some persons find sweetness in prayer but much difficulty in the practice of mortification, so they leave the bitter for the sweet, the laborious for the delightful, with the result that they spend all their time in prayer and little time in mortification. But the human heart is so drawn to self-satisfaction that there is a strong temptation to choose only what gives pleasure or even to commit sin in the pursuit of sensate satisfaction. And if one type of pleasure is denied, the human heart is so crafty that it will seek satisfaction in a substitute. Thus, the man who observes the vow of chastity will sometimes, unwittingly perhaps, seek sensate satisfaction in food or drink; the result is that he still has the vice of intemperance.

This self-centered love is what infects so many of our good deeds and prevents us from acting entirely out of the love of God. Many persons who pride themselves on their good deeds will discover, if they look closely, that in many instances they have acted out of selfish interests. Similarly, some of the people who are so eager to attend many Masses, listen to sermons, make novenas, etc., very readily give way to anger, pride, impatience, greed, or some other capital sin, which shows that they lack the virtues proper to the Christian life. It sometimes happens that persons who are so adamant about practicing their private devotions or even daily Mass and Communion are negligent in performing some of the duties of their state in life.

Let us return once again to the important matter of spiritual consolations, which may come from any one of three causes. First of all, they may come from the Holy Spirit, who uses them to wean us away from the things of earth and draw us towards the life of Christian virtue. Second, they may have a natural cause, as when they arise from tender and sensitive disposition of the individual or from the nature of the subject matter of one's meditation or contemplation. For example, to contemplate the beauties of God's creation was sufficient to move St. Francis of Assisi to sing the praises of God. Third, spiritual gifts and consolations may be the work of the devil, who uses these things to deceive individuals and make them think that they are very holy and highly favored.

Whatever the source of spiritual gifts and consolations, the person who receives them has no reason to think highly of himself solely on that account. If they are from the Holy Spirit, they should be received with humility and holy fear as instruments for growth in the love of God and neighbor. If they have a human cause, they are simply the concomitant effects of a purely natural contemplation which could be experienced by anyone who is properly disposed. And if they are the work of the devil, therein lies the danger of being deceived by the devil, who usually tempts devout persons under the guise of something virtuous and holy in order to lead them astray. One can see from this how important it is to discern the cause of spiritual phenomena and if that is not possible, to wait and judge from the effects they produce.

Devout souls who wish to be ever more closely united with God should follow the path of obedience, not only obeying his commandments, but striving to be responsive to his inspirations and actual graces. Although there is always a danger of misinterpreting the movements of grace, if a person follows the advice of St. John, he need not fear being deceived: "Do not trust every spirit, but put the spirits to a test to see if they belong to God" (1 Jn 4:1).

Moreover, one should always follow the general rule: when one has a choice of performing a work of obligation or one that is purely optional: that which is of obligation should always come first, however excellent and meritorious the optional work may be. As Samuel told Saul: "Obedience is better than sacrifice" (1 S 15:22).

- 17 -

The States of Life

MANY VIRTUES ARE REQUIRED for living the Christian life, but not all the virtues are equally necessary. Some devout souls will be outstanding in the practice of certain virtues and other souls will excel in other virtues. For example, persons who are drawn to the contemplative life will be characterized by the practice of prayer and recollection, the worship of God in the liturgy, and an asceticism of separation from the world and social contacts. Others, and they are the majority, will be better suited to the active life, which is dedicated to the service of others, the works of charity and the apostolate. Still others find that their Christian life is a blending of the active life and the contemplative life, which the ancient theologians called the "mixed life." Such is or should be the life of a teacher of sacred doctrine, a preacher, a bishop, or anyone who is called to the service of others in the ministry.

However, there is a very common error among Christians in regard to the practice of the various virtues proper to one of the three states of life: contemplative, active or mixed. Those who have made significant progress, for example, along the contemplative way will be inclined to think that such is the only way and will try to impose it on everyone else. Hence, the Christian who is able to spend long hours in prayer and recollection makes that the standard by which he measures all growth in holiness. He may even go so far as to criticize those who dedicate themselves to the active life of works of charity and the apostolate. On the other hand, since persons engaged in the active life can see immediate results of their apostolate, they may be tempted to look upon the contemplative life as a life of leisure and selfishness. They may even belittle the mixed life because of the time spent in prayer or the study of sacred doctrine, although the mixed life terminates in the apostolate or ministry.

Every tradesman praises his own wares, and everyone, either wittingly or unwittingly, favors that which is most beneficial to himself or that which he does best. The same thing is true as regards the practice of the virtues. The individual who reaps much benefit from mental prayer may be tempted to belittle vocal prayer as suitable only for children or the uneducated. The priest whose primary work is preaching or teaching may look with disdain at the parish priest. We find the same type of mentality among professors, when the theologian belittles the work of the canon lawyer. The same prejudices can be found in the secular professions.

We have to realize that the shoe that fits one person will not necessarily fit everyone else. Secondly, we should take to heart the teaching of St. Paul in Chapter 12 of the First Letter to the Corinthians, where he states that there is a variety of gifts but the one Holy Spirit, a diversity of graces but the same Spirit, a variety of ministries but the one Lord. "It is one and the same Spirit who produces all these gifts, distributing them to each as he wills" (1 Cor 12:11).

Then, comparing the Mystical Body of Christ, of which we are members, with the human body, St. Paul says: "The body is one and has many members, but all the members, many though they are, are one body. Now the body is not one member, it is many. If the foot should say, 'Because I am not a hand I do not belong to the body,' would it then no longer belong to the body? If the ear should say, 'Because I am not an eye I do not belong to the body,' would it then no longer belong to the body? If the body were all eye, what would happen to our hearing? If it were all ear, what would happen to our smelling?... You, then, are the body of Christ. Every one of you is a member of it" (1 Cor 12:12-20, 27).

There is, therefore, a certain unity among all the members of the Mystical Body, a unity of faith and one baptism by which all are incorporated into the Church of Christ. At the same time there is a certain diversity, depending on the gifts and graces received through the Holy Spirit and the particular vocation that God wills for each one. The very perfection and beauty of the Church require that there be a variety of gifts and ministries, as St. Paul teaches: "God has set up in the church first apostles, second prophets, third teachers, then, miracle workers, healers, assistants, administrators, and those who speak in tongues. Are all apostles? Are all prophets? Are all teachers? Do all work miracles or have the gift of healing? Do all speak in tongues, do all have the gift of interpretation of tongues? Set your hearts on the greater gifts.... There are in the end three things that last: faith, hope, and love, and the greatest of these is love" (1 Cor 12:28-31; 13:13).

Since variety is necessary for the beauty of the Church, why is it that we criticize one another because others do not live and act as we do? That is destructive of the unity of the Church, which is preserved by the bond of charity. It creates discord and divisiveness when one group condemns another for being different in their state of life, their liturgy, or in some other aspect of the Christian life. It is also a sign of ignorance or the inability or unwillingness to understand that the circumstances or needs of others are not the same as our own. That is like the eyes criticizing the feet because they cannot see, or the feet complaining about the eyes because they cannot walk.

Therefore, let us leave each one to follow his own personal vocation. And let us remember that the notes written on the lines of a sheet of music are as important as the notes written between the lines. The final admonition comes from

St. Paul: "That is why Christ died and came to life again, that he might be Lord of both the dead and the living. But you, how can you sit in judgment on your brother? Or you, how can you look down on your brother? We shall all have to appear before the judgment seat of God.... Every one of us will have to give an account of himself before God. Therefore we must no longer pass judgment on one another. Instead you should resolve to put no stumbling block or hindrance in your brother's way.... Let us, then, make it our aim to work for peace and to strengthen one another" (Rm 14:9-13, 10).